PUBLIC SCHOOLING AND
THE EDUCATION OF DEMOCRATIC CITIZENS

Public Schooling
and the Education
of Democratic Citizens

Richard M. Battistoni

University Press of Mississippi
JACKSON & LONDON

Library of Congress Cataloging-in-Publication Data

Battistoni, Richard M.
  Public schooling and the education of democratic
citizens.

  Includes index.
  1. Civics—Study and teaching (Secondary)—United
States. I. Title.
H62.5.U5B345 1985   320.473   85-9133
ISBN 0-87805-280-1

CONTENTS

PREFACE

THE IMPETUS FOR WRITING this book grew out of my concern over the passive character of contemporary citizenship in America. In teaching introductory political science courses to students both at Rutgers and Baylor University, I became increasingly aware of a severe deficiency in the civic training these students had received in high school. The idea that democratic political life involved active participation, certain cognitive skills, or affective loyalties, for instance, seemed foreign to these most recent graduates of America's "official" schools for citizenship. With the bicentennial of the American Constitution rapidly approaching, these deficiencies in citizen education seem all the more dismaying.

With these concerns in mind, my purpose is to examine current practices in the high schools as they affect citizen education, using as a foundation a theoretical understanding of the characteristics of democratic politics and citizenship as it has been handed down through the tradition of political philosophy. This study has given me a number of insights into why we produce the kinds of citizens we do, and has provided me with a number of ways to attempt in my own teaching to remedy current problems in the training of young citizens. It has also produced some surprises for me in terms of the evolution of my own thinking. Growing up during the Vietnam era, I did not appreciate, as I do now, the need for future citizens (regardless of their ultimate political leanings) to learn the substantive values of, or emotional bonding to, the political community.

It is not easy to do justice to those people who share in the responsibility for whatever merits this book has. I owe a great debt to those who read all or parts of the manuscript, and offered their counsel and criticism. In particular I want to acknowledge Benjamin Barber, who has been a part of this project from its very beginnings, where he played a major role in redirecting me to a more fruitful focus, to the final product, which has profited greatly from his textual comments and suggestions. His overall support made this whole process not only worthwhile but enjoyable. I also benefited from careful readings of all or parts of the manuscript by Carey McWilliams, Robert McClintock, Michael Sandel, Rob Smith, Garrett Sheldon, Laura Greyson, R. Freeman Butts, Gordon Schochet, and Clarke Cochran. These colleagues helped me to steer clear of a number of intellectual obstacles, and pointed out the ones that still remain due to my obstinacy in deciding not to heed their sound advice.

Baylor University has been generous with both its financial resources and its moral support—Robert T. Miller, my department chair, has been particularly supportive and encouraging.

A book about education cannot fail to acknowledge teachers and students. The graduate faculty at Rutgers University provided me with the solid intellectual training and the chance to participate in a community of scholars which has helped me become the teacher and scholar I wanted to be, and to them I owe a special debt. My high school "civics" teachers, Michael Juarez, James Schlude, and Michael Van Wert, all demonstrated in one way or another that civic learning in the high school classroom is possible. And Clarence Piggott, who not only taught me in high school but helped with some of the material on civics textbooks, showed me the kind of caring that makes the teacher-student relationship so special—a caring for which he gave his life, both figuratively and literally. My students at Baylor, particularly those who endured a version of my argument in a seminar in contemporary democratic theory in the spring of 1984, also deserve my sincere appreciation.

Special thanks go to Patricia Urbantke, who typed and retyped the manuscript with care and patience, and who has taught me all I know about using word processors.

And finally, I am most indebted to my wife, Betsy Ritz, whose intellectual and editorial assistance is responsible for much of the success of this manuscript, and whose love and friendship make the remaining failures bearable.

Waco, Texas
January 1985

PUBLIC SCHOOLING AND
THE EDUCATION OF DEMOCRATIC CITIZENS

The Crisis
in American Civic Education

We have physicists, geometricians, chemists, astronomers, poets, musicians, and painters in plenty; but we have no longer a citizen among us; or if there be found a few scattered over our abandoned countryside, they are left to perish there unnoticed and neglected.

Jean-Jacques Rousseau

EVERY MODERN POLITY engages in the practice of political education. In all modern societies, people must be taught the values underlying the social order and the workings of their political institutions before engaging in any sort of political activity, whether it be sustaining the status quo or reforming political practices. In one way or another, all political communities need to instill in their citizens basic feelings of political trust and loyalty to ensure the ongoing resilience of the fabric of the political order. Through a conscious civic education, society transforms individual members of the polity into citizens, thus enabling them to exercise their rights and perform their public duties. Since all of these qualities are not innate, and are not learned systematically in private spheres such as the family, they must be taught and learned under some type of public support and guidance.

Civic education is especially important to democratic societies. In a democracy, society's reliance on the people to make deliberate choices about the direction their collective lives and energies should take makes it crucial that the citizenry be educated. George Washington, in his farewell address, emphasized that "in proportion as the structure of a government gives force to public opinion, it is essential that public opinion should be enlightened."[1] Citizens need

3

to possess the cognitive skills and abilities necessary to responsibly participate in democratic politics. In addition, the rights and freedoms accorded in a democracy make it especially imperative that democratic states teach citizens the public responsibilities that go along with democratic rights, as well as the moral and cultural foundations which bind the political order together. Even those who would challenge the very foundations and institutions of particular democratic regimes have recognized the potential importance of political education as a precondition to radical social change (witness the growing number of Marxists involved in the study of political education, and not merely the "indoctrinational" or "hegemonic" aspects, but also the potentially liberating ones).

Given the importance of citizenship education to democratic societies, we would expect to find a coherent articulation of the form and content of American civic education, as well as concrete practices corresponding to such an articulation. Contemporary America, however, seems to be undergoing a crisis in civic education. Over the past twenty years there has been a continuous erosion of shared political values in American society. There is no longer a concern for "things political" among our nation's youth, nor a commitment to participate in the making of political decisions, at any level. Robert Pranger has argued that "the citizen, whose chief duty is to participate, is disappearing as an important political actor."[2] David Mathews, Secretary of Health, Education and Welfare during the mid-1970s, laid out the problem of citizenship education in this way:

> Being a citizen today is essentially a spectator sport. Citizenship education is little more than learning what others do to make and execute the policies of government. Citizenship cannot be remote. The disinterested citizen becomes disengaged, the disengaged citizen becomes disillusioned, and disillusionment leads to despair. We may well be witnessing the kind of citizen dropout that Thomas Jefferson imagined when he asked, in his first inaugural address, if the American experiment in self-government might be withering for lack of energy to sustain it.[3]

The cause for alarm stems from the seeming failure of the major "agents" of citizenship education in America to respond to our current crisis. A study of Pennsylvania high school seniors in 1974 showed their understanding of democracy to be simplistic and shallow, and this after having recently completed high school civics instruction. The overwhelming majority of these students believed "the main characteristic of democracy was that it leaves the citizen alone." In addition, these seniors were unable to apply "democratic ideas" to concrete situations where conflict or an active, participatory response was demanded.[4] Further, a national cross-section of 30-year-olds studied periodically from 1960 to 1976 found one of the "glaring shortcomings" of the nation's high schools to be the "ineffective education for citizenship in a democratic society."[5]

Political socialization studies have found that all three of the major "agents" of American citizenship education—the schools, the family, and the communications media—generally have been unable to instill political values or the necessary norms of political activity in future citizens.[6] The very fact that political scientists talk about "political socialization" (which, unlike "political education," tends to focus on more casual learning and the *latent* internalization of social and political attitudes) indicates that we have abandoned the idea that any agent in modern liberal democracies can *consciously and directly* educate active democratic citizens. Moreover, the fact that many schools give grades for "citizenship" based on a student's neatness, politeness, submission of homework on time, and passive obedience to school rules suggests that our educators have forgotten what it means to be a democratic citizen.

Indeed, the events of the past decades have accelerated our society's declining capacity to teach citizen norms and skills, especially in the schools. The launching of Sputnik by the Soviet Union in 1957 caused a national response in the late 1950s and 1960s that emphasized technical and specialized education in secondary schools. Achievement in mathematics and the sciences was stressed over other traditional subjects in the humanities. Education was increasingly held to be important to reach personal and technical national goals, but the general goal of developing better citizens was not directly addressed in this period.

Beginning in the late 1960s and continuing into the present, public officials have started to address the problems of discrimination, unequal opportunity, and "free choice" in education. In the last fifteen years, the courts have been used increasingly to eliminate inequalities and discriminatory practices and to challenge certain mandatory practices in the schools. Issues such as sexual and racial discrimination, school busing, student rights, school prayer, and compulsory school attendance have all been subjects of recent litigation in various courts across the country.

The increasingly litigious and legalistic nature of the public schools, and especially secondary schools, has not contributed to overcoming the current crisis in civic education. The increasing option of recourse to the courts and the judicial process in educational matters signals (along with a complete distrust of public authority) a failure to maintain or achieve any community of meaning in the schools. Some may see the growing use of the courts as a sign of the return of politics to the schools. But legal actions of this sort have served only to further fragment and factionalize different groups within the school, dividing students, teachers, and parents into different classes and interests. The involvement of the courts in the schools educates future citizens only as to their differences, their separation from one another, and their rights as separate entities; it does not teach common values or public responsibilities.[7]

Currently, there seems to be a desire to return to the immediate post-Sputnik era. Concerns over the failures of our nation's schools, most recently generated by a number of much-heralded reports, including that of the President's National Commission on Excellence in Education,[8] have yielded a number of policy proposals for upgrading mathematics and science instruction and for rewarding merit in teaching. While these proposals will undoubtedly contribute to improvements in the overall system of American education, few specific comments or proposals have been made regarding the improvement of *civic education* in American schools.

Of the major reports issued in 1983, only those of the Carnegie Foundation and the Twentieth Century Fund explicitly acknowledge the fact that civic education ought to be one of the foremost concerns of the schools.[9] The President's Commission on Excellence in Education addresses the question of citizenship education, but only indirectly and superficially. It offers no concrete discussion of the specific skills or values necessary for responsible democratic citizenship nor the kinds of programs that would contribute to them. With the exception of the Commission's brief discussion of high school social studies requirements, there is very little mention of the actual goals of citizenship education of American high schools. Most importantly, public discussion of all these reports (particularly in the news media) has centered on overall individual achievement and proficiency in technical education, much as was the case during the late 1950s and 1960s.[10]

And yet, without proper attention to civic education, America will not produce the kinds of citizens who will propose and support public programs meant to accomplish even these specific technical and achievement goals. That is, without an understanding of the common purposes upon which public programs are pursued (such understanding coming at least in part from a solid instruction in civics), there may be no agreement among private citizens about what collective efforts are necessary and appropriate to improve our community's schools.

The current capacity of our schools for teaching the lessons of democratic citizenship is indeed limited. A recent examination of contemporary high schools yielded this ominous characterization:

> In the past generation the older sources of authority and consensus have been severely challenged. Within the system a once united professional front has crumbled as teachers, administrators, and other staff have waged internecine battle. Many groups—students, minorities, women, the handicapped, school finance reformers—have found the law a ready instrument for change. Older processes of political accommodation of differences have eroded as aggrieved parties turned to the courts. To meet the needs of underserved students, federal and state categorical programs have proliferated, all demanding new forms of accountability. Webs of regulations and paperwork empires prescribe the forms and processes of schooling, circumscribing the autonomy of local educators, turning many of them into social accountants.[11]

Many educators find themselves in "a state of shock and overload" from these developments in the schools. The dean of Stanford's School of Education has gone so far as to argue that "for the first time, it is conceivable to envision the dismantling of universal, public, compulsory education as it has been pioneered in America."[12]

The Failures of Political Socialization Research

The situation with respect to citizenship education in America seems critical. And as we have just detailed above, the developments in school goals and policy over the past twenty-five years do not bode well for our future ability to revive the schools as civic educators. But there has been a potentially positive development at least in the scholarship relating to political education in the past twenty-five years. In this period political socialization has emerged as an increasingly important field of study. What have studies in political socialization contributed to our knowledge about citizen education, and how can they assist us in possibly solving the current crisis?

Some of the findings of political socialization research have direct implications for the future of civic education in America. As mentioned earlier, socialization research indicates that, contrary to popular belief, the major agents of political socialization have had a limited impact in terms of direct and conscious inculcation of democratic norms and attitudes. With respect to the high schools in particular, while it is still believed that they are important political socializers, "it has been very difficult to pinpoint exactly which properties of the school are crucial in the socialization process."[13]

It seems clear from the research, however, that high school government courses and the civics curriculum in general, "at least as these are presently constituted," have very minimal impact as "a major source of political socialization."[14] Students have been found to exhibit very limited improvement in political knowledge or in democratic political attitudes after taking high school civics courses. Studies have shown that the type of political education that students get from their high school civics curriculum fails effectively to link cognitive (intellectual and reasoning skills) with affective (emotional ties and bonds to the political community) lessons of citizenship.[15] Moreover, researchers have concluded that informal norms and customary methods and practices in the school (often termed the "hidden curriculum") may have a greater impact than the formal curriculum on what students learn about citizenship.[16]

We have learned from political socialization research that, as far as secondary schools are concerned, a "radical restructuring" of the civics curriculum, so that it pays attention to the overall "high school experience" and not just to the content of formal civics courses, may be able to bring about substantial gains in civic learning.[17] By looking at the results of particular socialization studies, educators potentially can find out what curricular practices need rethinking and innovation. This has been the major contribution of political socialization research.

For the most part, however, political socialization studies have failed to illuminate the problems in American civic instruction or to lead us to specific solutions to these problems. Many socialization studies, especially the earliest ones, primarily concentrated on explaining the persistence of support for the political status quo in children's learning.[18] The questions many researchers asked were structured by concerns for the continued functioning of the political system, not with the individual's political learning process. One scholar has even defined political socialization as solely involving "the process by which people learn to adopt the norms, values, attitudes and behaviors *accepted and practiced by the ongoing system* (emphasis added)."[19] The focus of many of these socialization studies on such "macro-level questions" as diffuse systemic support has needlessly narrowed their vision and impact.

In addition, political socialization studies generally have been flawed in their methods of examining the question of citizenship education. Studies have tended to look more closely at the "who" (the agents involved and their relative impact) than the "what" (the actual process of political learning, its content, and patterns of interaction between child and agent) of political socialization. Research has centered on how young people model their political attitudes along the lines of the various agents they encounter, whether they be parents or teachers. Political scientists and sociologists studying political socialization have taken "snapshot" pictures of the degree of agreement between students and parents, teachers, or peers on various measures of political attitudes, rather than doing detailed observations of the process of interaction between children, institutions of political learning, and authority figures responsible for teaching them political lessons.[20]

For example, one of the more influential studies of the effects of the secondary school, its curriculum, and teachers upon the political socialization of adolescents (Jennings and Niemi, *The Political Character of Adolescence*) focuses on attitude agreement between educational agents and students, to the neglect of other critical questions. In exploring the effects of the civics curriculum, the Jennings and Niemi study takes an attitudinal "snapshot" of students both before and after having taken one government course (sometimes two). From this they conclude that in most cases the curriculum has a minimal effect. They do not look at course or textbook content, nor at the larger high school curriculum and its possible effects on citizen education.

In examining the impact of the teacher on students' political attitudes, Jennings and Niemi pair students with their civics teacher, and measure agreement between the paired groups on items such as partisan identification and intensity, political efficacy and trust scales, and particular political issues of the day.[21] They pay no attention to the nuances of classroom interaction or to teacher style or method. The study merely looks, in a vacuum, at the student's relationship with one or two teachers, based upon a narrowly conceived model of authority relationships and attitude agreement. While Jennings and Niemi admit to the "virtue of examining the finer grain of teacher performance and course content,"[22] their study of the effects of the school on political learning goes on without any further concern for this "virtue"!

Furthermore, the study follows the path of most other socialization studies in focusing solely on the learning of specific political *attitudes.* Their research does not explore the role of the school and its curriculum in developing students' "political cognitions, skills and information," not to mention the possible development of affective ties toward the political order and other citizens.[23] The learning of cognitive and participatory skills in the schools, two seemingly crucial components of democratic citizenship education, is not studied at all. Moreover, a student's "political knowledge" is measured by a six-item test which is remarkable only in its simplicity and its irrelevance to larger questions of citizenship.[24]

This is not to denigrate one particular study in political socialization, which nevertheless has its merits, but rather to give an example of what is wrong with the entire field of research. For methodological as well as conceptual reasons, researchers in political socialization have not asked the most important questions about citizen education in America. It has been easier for them to conduct attitude surveys of children, parents, and teachers than to examine the content or process of political socialization or the structures of socializing institutions and their impact on political learning. Even methodological approaches like participant observation and quasi-experimental designs, which might be able to get at more subtle or in-depth information about the political socialization process, have been rejected in favor of a narrowly conceived survey research approach. As a result, the political socialization literature "cannot and will not tell us what ought to be taught" in terms of citizenship education, nor "how it should be taught." Richard Merelman contends that political socialization research should not even "be expected to yield a theory of social studies teaching."[25] Furthermore, since the political socialization literature does not ask the primary theoretical question of what it really means to be a democratic citizen, interested educators and students of politics have no criteria by which to judge the findings that socialization research *has* yielded. Political socialization researchers have not taken heed of a much earlier tradition in the study of politics, which understands that "it is necessary to know what *ought to be* in order to judge soundly about what *is*."[26]

It is in light of our contemporary crisis in political education and of the failure of research in political science to address this crisis properly that this project is undertaken. The question of American political education will be addressed by looking first to the tradition of political philosophy to examine two different "conceptions" or "models" of democratic politics and citizenship. We want to find out what qualities constitute democratic citizenship under each model, and how in general terms each conceives of the role of education in creating democratic citizens. After examining the question of democratic citizenship theoretically, I will move on to consider specific practices in the schools which affect the education of citizens. My specific focus will be on problems in contemporary school practices in the following areas: the content and methods in the civics curriculum, both explicit and implicit; the structure of educational institutions; and the role of the teacher—all as they relate to civic education, and all in light of the prior theoretical discussion of what it means to be a democratic citizen under the two established models. By proceeding in this way, I hope to explore the ramifications of school policies and practices for citizenship training, and point the direction to changes that can be made in such practices.

The reason for focusing on the schools as civic educators is twofold. First of all, the schools are involved in the conscious instilling of values, skills, and knowledge relevant to citizenship. Although the schools teach many "latent lessons" of citizenship as well (through the "hidden curriculum" and the general structure of educational institutions—see Part II), the schools more than any other educational agent in contemporary America attempt directly and formally to teach their students lessons in democratic citizenship. Families, peers, and the mass media, though also potentially important agents of political education, are not systematically and directly responsible for the inculcation of citizen norms. When they do teach important political lessons, they often do so unconsciously. Charles Merriam, in his eight-nation study, *The Making of Citizens,* called the school "the major instrument in the shaping of civic education . . . the heart of the civic education of the political community."²⁷ This is not to say that education is synonymous with schooling, or that civic learning does not go on outside of the schools, but merely that the schools must be the major focus of any discussion of citizenship education.

The importance of the schools in citizen education is made even more manifest by evidence of the erosion of many of the schools' societal supplements in recent years. The family, local communities, religious institutions, and the workplace have all relinquished their roles as significant civic instructors in contemporary American life. It is the schools that now attract both the hopes and the criticisms of those concerned with citizenship education.

Should there be a complete absence of conscious citizen training in schools, the young will be "socialized" by society in general and by the communications media, whose view of politics is laced with cynicism and disdain. The generations of the '70s and '80s are becoming increasingly alienated by political events and how they are reported in the media. By engaging in a counterpoint, in a conscious discussion of political values and ideals in the wake of contemporary political events, schools may be able to maintain active citizenship among the young. In the absence of schools taking a direct and systematic role, we will see only further political withdrawal and despair.

This brings us to the second reason for a focus on public schooling in America. Of all the agents of political education in American society, the school is the only one that can be significantly manipulated by political practice. Unlike the family or other more private institutions in society, a discussion of problems in the schools as they affect citizen education can be the object of public policy debate and reform. Given the public nature of their activity and the comparatively easy access citizens can have to schools, serious thinking about how we educate democratic citizens can be translated into changes in the practices of the schools more easily than in the practices of the family or other social institutions.[28]

John Dewey understood why reformers should focus their attentions on the schools when talking about changes in the way citizens interact and are organized for social purposes:

> By law and punishment, by social agitation and discussion, society can regulate and form itself in a more or less haphazard and chance way. But through *education* society can formulate its own purposes, can organize its own means and resources, and thus shape itself with definiteness and economy in the direction in which it wishes to move.[29]

Dewey even contended that the schools could be catalysts in transforming social and political relations in general. He felt that Americans must

> make each one of our schools an embryonic community life, active with types of occupations that reflect the life of the larger society, and permeated throughout with the spirit of art, history, and science. When the school introduces and trains each child of society into membership within such a little community, saturating him with the spirit of service, and providing him with the instruments of effective self-direction, we shall have the deepest and best guarantee of a larger society which is worthy, lovely, and harmonious.[30]

This examination of the schools and their practices will concentrate on the high schools in particular. While some of the earlier political socialization studies have shown that the most important adult political attitudes are learned early in childhood, the bulk of more recent research has revealed that attitudes learned early in childhood are extremely general and show great instability over time. One study contends that sometime in adolescence attitudes toward authority change from those acquired in childhood. The adolescent individual begins to see political authorities as accountable, and invests the notion of authority with a strong participatory element, where only benevolence and unquestioned loyalty accompanied the younger child's vision of authority.[31] More recent political socialization studies show that it is only beginning with adolescence that lessons and attitudes more specific to adult political behavior are learned and persist in individuals.[32]

In addition, research in cognitive development has shown that not until adolescence are most children capable of abstract or sociocentric thought, and thus able to grasp lessons of citizenship at all cognitive levels. Only beginning with adolescence do students achieve cognitive levels appropriate to perceiving and discussing ideas and images, and to giving meaning to their disparate experiences. For these reasons, then, only at the high school level can we adequately deal with the wide range of topics that make up an effective discussion about the civics curriculum.[33]

Furthermore, not until high school does direct study in "civics" assume sophisticated proportions. Only at the secondary school level do states and localities mandate some form of intensive civics or social studies instruction to provide for the education of youth in the lessons of future citizenship.

Moreover, it has been argued that the high schools will increasingly be the major focus of criticism and reform from a number of diverse groups. The high school student's relative physical and intellectual maturity (which creates the benefits of receptivity to higher levels of learning as well as the burdens of authority and control) as well as the proximity of the high school to society at large make it a prime target for both fundamentalists and radical "free-schoolers." And the complexity and atomization of the administration and curriculum at the high school level make it easier to propose and implement piecemeal changes. Many would agree with Sidney Marland, the former U.S. Commissioner of Education, who sees the high school as "a troubled institution and the most likely arena of educational change for the balance of this decade. While there is dissatisfaction, frustration, and readiness for change throughout all of education, the opportunities for reform are especially timely in high school."[34]

My purpose will be to draw on the contributions of many of the classical political thinkers in our Western tradition in exploring the problem of contemporary citizenship education in American secondary schools. Part I will consist of a detailed discussion of two distinct conceptions of democratic politics, citizenship, and political education which have been culled from the tradition of political thought. Part II will consider the question of how we go about educating democratic citizens, using models of what it means to be a democratic citizen to illuminate current curricular practices in American high schools.

Our current crisis in civic education is severe. Ernest Boyer has argued that "unless we find better ways to educate ourselves as citizens we run the risk of drifting unwittingly into a new kind of Dark Age."[35] Part of the reason we have arrived at this crossroads in democratic citizenship is that we have assumed for a number of years that democracy "happens" by itself, without any conscious struggle or recommitment to its ideals. We have taken democracy and democratic citizenship for granted. What we must understand once again is that a vibrant democracy must continually be created and recreated, and that crucial to its creation is the proper inculcation in the young of the character, skills, values, social practices, and ideals that foster democratic politics. As mentioned at the outset, all democratic societies must engage in such educational practices; our attempt to avoid conscious instruction for fear of trampling on "freedom" is foolish. The question, as one writer has put it, "is not *whether* but *how* one cultivates the necessary moral virtue, the sense of civic responsibility, and the reflective commitment to democratic traditions that sustain a democratic culture."[36] It is to this question in all of its complexity that we must now turn.

NOTES

1. Quoted in Sheldon Wolin, "Higher Education and the Politics of Knowledge," *democracy* 1, no. 2 (April 1981): 38.
2. Robert Pranger, *The Eclipse of Citizenship* (New York: Holt, Rinehart, and Winston, 1968), 3.

3. B. Frank Brown, "The Case for Citizenship Education," in *Education for Responsible Citizenship: The Report of the National Task Force on Citizenship Education* (New York: McGraw-Hill, 1977), 3.

4. Roberta Sigel, "Students' Comprehension of Democracy and Its Application to Conflict Situations," *International Journal of Political Education* 2 (1979): 46–65.

5. A. Harry Passow, *Secondary Education Reform: Retrospect and Prospect* (New York: Teachers College Press, 1976), 7.

6. See for example Roberta S. Sigel and Marilyn B. Hoskin, *The Political Involvement of Adolescents* (New Brunswick: Rutgers University Press, 1981); M. Kent Jennings and Richard G. Niemi, *The Political Character of Adolescence* (Princeton: Princeton University Press, 1974); Paul Beck, "The Role of Agents in Political Socialization," in Stanley Renshon, ed., *Handbook of Political Socialization* (New York: The Free Press, 1977), 115–141.

7. See Gerald Grant, "The Character of Education and the Education of Character," *Daedalus* (Summer 1981): 140–144; David Tyack and Elizabeth Hansot, "Conflict and Consensus in American Public Education," *Daedalus* (Summer 1981): 19. Tyack and Hansot contend that categorical federal and state programs also tend to divide groups in the schools.

8. *A Nation At Risk: The Imperative for Educational Reform*, (Washington: U.S. Department of Education, 1983).

9. Ernest L. Boyer, *High School: A Report on Secondary Education in America* (New York: Harper & Row, Publishers, 1983); *Task Force on Federal Elementary and Secondary Education Policy* (Twentieth Century Foundation, 1983).

10. President Reagan overlooked his own commission's discussions of the civic purposes of public education in making his recommendations for education reform based on their report. For a similar argument to the one I'm making, see R. Freeman Butts, "Attending to the Civic Mission of American Education," *Kettering Review* (Winter 1984): 24–27.

11. Tyack and Hansot, "Conflict and Consensus," 15.

12. "Help! Teacher Can't Teach!", *Time* (June 16, 1980), 54.

13. Jennings and Niemi, *Political Character of Adolescence*, 328.

14. Ibid., 190–191, 205. See also Richard Merelman, "The Adolescence of Political Socialization," *Sociology of Education* 45, no. 2 (1972): 134–166.

15. Sigel and Hoskin, *Political Involvement of Adolescents*, 123–28.

16. Richard Merelman, "Democratic Politics and the Culture of American Education," *American Political Science Review* 74, no. 2 (June 1980): 319–31.

17. Jennings and Niemi, *Political Character of Adolescence*; Merelman, "Democratic Politics"; John J. Patrick, "Political Socialization and Political Education in Schools," in Renshon, *Handbook of Political Socialization*, 190–222.

18. Prime examples of these are David Easton and Jack Dennis, *Children in the Political System: Origins of Political Legitimacy* (New York: McGraw-Hill, 1969); Fred Greenstein, *Children and Politics* (New Haven: Yale University Press, 1965); Robert Hess and Judith Torney, *The Development of Political Attitudes in Children* (Chicago: Aldine Press, 1967).

19. Roberta Sigel, *Learning About Politics: A Reader in Political Socialization* (New York: Random House, 1970), xii.

20. Methodological arguments about the dangers of concluding *anything* from such "snapshot" pictures and about problems with reactivity inherent in the testing situation can be found in B. Marsh, "Political Socialization: The Implicit Assumptions Examined," *British Journal of Political Science* (October 1971): 453–465, and Merelman, "The Adolescence of Political Socialization."

21. Jennings and Niemi, *Political Character of Adolescence,* 207–227.

22. Ibid., 193.

23. They also admit that this part of political learning is "scarcely undertaken here" (in their research); Ibid., 328.

24. The six questions this survey asked about politics were: 1) the governor of the respondent's state, 2) the country with concentration camps in World War II, 3) whether Franklin Roosevelt was a Democrat or a Republican, 4) the length of a senator's term, 5) the number of justices on the Supreme Court, and 6) the country of which Tito is the leader.

25. Merelman, "The Adolescence of Political Socialization," 162.

26. Jean-Jacques Rousseau, *Emile,* Allan Bloom, trans. (New York: Basic Books, 1979), 458.

27. Quoted in Judith Torney, et al., *Civic Education in Ten Countries* (New York: John Wiley and Sons, 1975), 30.

28. The truth of this assumption is borne out by the report of the Commission on Excellence in Education, whose findings have triggered a number of plans for changes in American schools.

29. John Dewey, "My Pedagogical Creed," in *Dewey on Education,* ed. Martin S. Dworkin, (New York: Teachers College Press, 1959), 31.

30. John Dewey, *The School and Society* (Chicago: University of Chicago Press, 1956), 43–44.

31. Richard E. Dawson, Kenneth Prewitt, and Karen S. Dawson, *Political Socialization* (Boston: Little, Brown, and Co., 1977), 207–12.

32. Sigel and Hoskin, *Political Involvement of Adolescents;* Marsh, "Political Socialization"; R. W. Connell, "Political Socialization and the American Family: The Evidence Re-examined," *Public Opinion Quarterly* 36 (Fall 1972): 323–333.

33. In addition, certain affective traits important to citizenship can only be learned in high schools since, as Royce argued, "the age for true and systematic loyalty can hardly precede adolescence"; Josiah Royce, "The Philosophy of Loyalty," *Basic Writings,* vol. 2 (Chicago: University of Chicago Press, 1969), 958.

34. Quoted in Passow, *Secondary Education Reform,* 29. *Daedalus* recently devoted two issues (Summer and Fall 1981) to problems and prospects in the nation's schools, and decided to focus on high schools in particular. And the National Commission on Excellence in Education's recent report on the status of contemporary American education also chose to focus its findings and recommendations on high schools. However, the paradox of concentrating on high schools as the most likely candidates for criticism and reform proposals is that reform, though more frequently proposed, has been usually less quick in coming in secondary schools than in elementary schools. Some of the reasons for this are that they are more complex institutions, their students more psychologically mature, with well-defined interests and greater independence. High school students have much greater exposure to outside influences as well, and the fact that they are harder to control (due to all of these factors) makes the high schools stress discipline, order, and conformity rather than change and innovation; see Charles Silberman, *Crisis in the Classroom: The Remaking of American Education* (New York: Random House, 1970), 324–25.

35. Boyer, *High School,* 105.

36. J. Peter Euben, "Philosophy and the Professions," *democracy* 1, no. 2 (April 1981): 126–27.

PART I

Two Conceptions
of Democratic Citizenship

OUR PURPOSE is to inquire into the proper education of democratic citizens, given the contemporary crisis in political education
just discussed. Before this inquiry can be conducted, however, we
need to know what it means to be a democratic citizen. Although
there are a number of different understandings of democratic politics that can be gleaned from the tradition of political thought, there
seem to be two general conceptions of the democratic citizen which
predominate. These two views, which I call the "liberal" and the
"participatory-republican" conceptions, contain competing theories
of human psychology and of the structure, scope, and function of
politics and government. Correspondingly, there follows a liberal
and participatory-republican notion of the general nature and function of political education.[1]

CHAPTER 1

The Liberal Conception
of the Democratic Citizen

THE LIBERAL CONCEPTION of democratic politics and citizenship begins with observations from psychology and epistemology. An examination of liberal notions about the self and the nature of its knowledge is important because the picture of the liberal individual that emerges helps us to understand the origins and function of liberal politics. After this explanation of the liberal depiction of human nature, the reasons for the artifices of politics and education will become clearer.

Liberal Psychology and the Origins of Politics

The liberal conception of the human psyche is based upon the fundamental premises of psychological hedonism and individualism. Jeremy Bentham argued that people are moved by their desires, pain and pleasure being the prime movers:

> Nature has placed mankind under the governance of two sovereign masters, pain and pleasure. It is for them to point out what we ought to do, as well as to determine what we shall do. . . . They govern us in all we do, in all we say, in all we think.[2]

For liberals, the motive for doing anything ultimately "is always some pleasure or some pain,"[3] and the desires "do continue constantly to operate and influence all our actions without ceasing."[4]

These motivating forces, however, are multiple, personal, and particular. Our desires are constantly changing, being modified or increased, and are fundamentally subjective. Given the particularistic nature of desire as the primary psychological motivation of human behavior, there can be no ready agreement as to the proper ordering among the passions, either between individuals or even within the individual him- or herself.[5] To complicate matters, the other faculties of the psyche, reason and will, which might provide a resolution to the anarchy of human wants and needs, are impotent because, according to the liberal position, these other faculties operate solely as appendages to the desires.

According to this liberal theory of the self, reason, which might teach us universal maxims, is not a general orderer or director of the passions but is subjective, a mere servant of the desires. Under liberal psychology, in fact, the relationship between reason and desire is one of subjection: desire is a blind and hungry mover of our mental processes; reason only serves to execute desire's designs. Thomas Hobbes says, "The thoughts are to the desires, as scouts, and spies, to range abroad and find the way to the things desired."[6]

In addition, reason is grossly insufficient as a motivation to action in the face of the desires. Liberal individuals cannot possibly direct their activity (let alone discuss with others the proper direction of community activity) through reason, as their passions are too powerful. Alexander Hamilton understood that "momentary passions and immediate interests have a more active and imperious control over human conduct than general or remote considerations of policy, utility, or justice."[7]

Epistemologically, reason also fails to offer a way out of the quandary of subjective knowledge. Reason cannot offer a route to objective truth or the "laws of nature," since the individual nature of perception of knowledge and the subjective nature of experience will not allow such objectivity. For Locke, reason is a faculty which "is necessary and assisting to all our other intellectual faculties" and can deduce and make connections among ideas and perceptions, but does not initiate anything in the quest for intersubjective knowledge. Reason "comes far short of the real extent of even corporeal being" and in "many instances" may "fail us" in our attempts to arrive at any standard of truth or knowledge.[8] Reason offers no resolution for liberals, either psychologically or epistemologically, to the subjectivity of human wants, needs, and experience.

The faculty of the *will* also fails to provide an adequate solution to the problem of maintaining an ordered and coherent personality in light of the fleeting nature of desires as the immediate cues to behavior. Under the liberal conception, the will is not an independent source of behavioral "advice" to the self, nor is it even a mediator between universal reason and particular passions. Will, like reason, is either attached to subjective appetites or is itself an appetite. For Hobbes, will is the last appetite, in deliberating over the course of action to take, that leads to an act of "doing or omitting."[9] And John Locke, though he places greater emphasis on the will than does Hobbes, ultimately sees the will as less a mediating ethical faculty than one determined by desire: "That which immediately determines the will, from time to time, to every voluntary action, is the uneasiness of desire, fixed on some absent good, either negative, as indolence to one in pain; or positive, as enjoyment of pleasure."[10] So although will is not *merely* an appetite for Locke, it is still directed by the appetitive forces of pleasure and pain.

At this juncture, the liberal theory of the self is left with the isolated individual as the primary standard of morality and truth. Since we are all motivated by desires, which are inherently personal and subjective, and since neither reason nor the will can offer a way out of this solipsistic universe, liberals like Locke are forced to equate "the good" or "virtue" with individual interest: "What has an aptness to produce pleasure in us is that we call *good,* and what is apt to produce pain in us we call *evil,* for no other reason but for its aptness to produce pleasure and pain in us."[11]

Women and men may be similar in their passions—they all desire, fear, hope, love—but not in the objects of their passions. For liberals, what distinguishes men and women from one another is not that they see or understand the world differently (though they may), but that they desire different things even when they share an identical vision or understanding of the world around them, or that they judge things around them differently, due to their particular interests. Locke contends that "we generally have different prospects of the same thing according to our different, as I may say, positions to it."[12]

In summary, then, the liberal conception of human psychology as I have drawn it here sees people as inherently isolated due to the ultimate subjectivity of human wants and interests. There can be no inherently legitimate common standard of good and evil, since there is no correct intersubjective ordering of our subjective interests. This isolation has clear implications for politics. The public realm requires a common language and a common set of rules governing action, as well as some agreed-upon goals that the polity will pursue. But since under the liberal conception an individual's interests are particularistic, they cannot be defended in the universal language of reason or public rhetoric. Due to the subjectivity of desires, men and women are fundamentally private beings, since they cannot offer others more than a "partial justification for their goals in the public language of thought."[13] Under the liberal model, ends are inevitably private.

There is for the liberal, however, one common good: power. Power is the means by which individuals secure and satisfy their desires, and since our greatest good is a sure and steady progression toward the objects of our desires with the least amount of hindrance, power is something all people always need. And since power to secure our future interests is always uncertain, men and women must engage in what Hobbes labeled "a perpetual and restless desire of power after power that ceaseth only in death."[14]

This drive for power necessarily affects all social relations, so that the basic liberal psychology, led out of the individual self into social interaction, turns into a more complex psychology of power-seeking, mastery, and domination. Given the subjective nature of the human psyche and the consequent striving for power to secure one's interests, women and men will constantly try to dominate and subjugate others in their own interest if not mediated or suppressed by some *disinterested* third party. For Locke, the potentially peaceful State of Nature degenerates into a State of War because each interested individual "attempts to get another man into his absolute power and use [him] as he pleases," ultimately to "make [him] a slave."[15]

Conflict between individuals ensues from all of this. A climate of fear, where people are distrustful of one another, antagonistic toward their neighbors and fellows, is bound to arise. The logic of the liberal psychology clearly demands some kind of public or political order which can act as a thunderstorm to wash away the oppressive humidity this climate of fear and uncertainty creates. But any public order is problematic, given that "most men prefer their private advantage to the public."[16] Moreover, as discussed earlier, people's interests, opinions, and even their responses to worldly "facts" will differ according to their different characters and wants, personal environments, and life experiences. The cruel irony is that as the problem of public order becomes more pressing due to increasing numbers of people in society striving for gain and the power to secure it, the attainment of any common rules of behavior becomes more difficult. Walter Lippmann saw this as especially true of twentieth-century democratic societies: "As the audience grows larger, the number of *common words* diminishes."[17]

So the political problem for liberals is to create a political order which both regulates the anarchy of subjective human activity and yet allows the individual the greatest possible purview to choose his or her own particular ends and the means of satisfying them. The liberal psychology leads us to the question of how to create a *legitimate* political order, given the liberal conception of human beings.

Liberal Politics
and the Problem of Legitimate Order

The liberal conception of politics and the proper political order begins with Locke's admission that "the only interests which a man at all times and upon all occasions is sure to find *adequate* motives for consulting, are his own."[18] The liberal psychology leaves us with people "busied about their private interest, and careless of what tends to the public."[19] Because these individuals cannot naturally moderate their own desires through general maxims that respect the desires of others, the artifice of politics and government becomes necessary. Since they cannot rule themselves, people must "put on the bonds of civil society." Hobbes says,

If men could rule themselves, every man by his own command, that is
to say, could they live according to the laws of nature, there would be
no need at all of a city, nor of a common coercive power.[20]

Without some type of political order, the enjoyment of our freedoms and rights is uncertain and exposed to invasion by others.
Conflicts arising from private judgments over matters of individual
right (especially rights to property) and from struggles over private
power would leave our enjoyment of life insecure in the absence of a
public mediator. In addition, James Madison felt that because "the
reason of man is fallible," and because there is an intimate connection "between his reason and his self-love," "different opinions will
be formed" about public policy. This "diversity in the faculty and
opinions of men" makes a unity of interests impossible, and institutions of government are needed to attempt to reach some form of
commonality with which all can be satisfied.[21]

Given this necessity, government for liberals is ideally envisioned
as the region of general, impersonal laws and disinterested judges,
where the inevitable conflicts between individuals are resolved.
Locke articulates this principle nicely, saying that "men being
biassed by their interest . . . are not apt to allow of [the law of
nature] as a law binding to them in the application of it to their
particular cases," and that unbiased judges or mediators are called
for since "men being partial to themselves, Passion and Revenge is
apt to carry them too far."[22] This liberal notion of the ideal government as an unbiased or impartial mediator between conflicting interests is consistent throughout liberal writers, from Hobbes and
Locke down to contemporary liberals such as Rawls.[23]

Under the liberal conception, politics and political activity are
purely instrumental. Individuals enter into politics "only with an
intention in every one the better to preserve himself his liberty and
property."[24] In fact, liberals argue that it would be folly to assume
that people "would quit the freedom of the State of Nature [to] tie
themselves up under [government], were it not to preserve their
lives, liberties and fortunes; and by *stated* rules of right and property secure their peace and quiet."[25] Under the liberal conception,
the polity is never seen as a source of values in its own right; all
values emanate from private individuals. There may be a sharing of
values or purposes in the polity, but this is better understood as a

coalition of interests which is contingent, and indeed precarious, given the subjectivity of interest.

For the liberal, then, political life is not sought out for its own sake, but only in so far as it offers private gain or profit. Liberal individuals do not particularly care to be influential in public affairs. They enter the political realm to secure their private needs, the goal being the "peaceful enjoyment of private independence"—but they remain psychologically isolated. Bonds between people in the polity are purely formal and ultimately based upon self-interest. Political participation is not a self-fulfilling or even a necessary activity; as long as one's private interests are represented one need not act any further in the public realm—in fact, such additional activity is foolish.[26]

Though politics is valued only as an expedient for the liberal, the political order is still needed to ensure that the individual can carve out his or her own path to private happiness through the provision and enforcement of common rules which secure the enjoyment of private interests. Political participation is not an inherent activity of the truly fulfilled self. Nevertheless, most liberals call for some form of democratic rule. Given that they clearly do not believe that political activity is of any intrinsic value to individual citizens, why would they advocate a political system calling for equal and universal citizen participation? What is the status of democracy under the liberal conception?

Democracy as a political form is preferred by liberals only because of the subjectivity of people's desires and the equality of their claims for the satisfaction of such desires. We have different interests and different opinions about what the public realm should do in accordance with those interests. Since no opinion is inherently "right" or "wrong," we all deserve an equal say in the final form of any public resolution of our differences. Our participation in politics is more of a defensive strategy than a self-fulfilling activity. Democracy is necessary only because it gives equal protection to individuals against incursions on their rights or interests by possibly arbitrary decrees of self-interested rulers. According to Rawls, democratic government exists to make sure "those in authority be responsive to the felt interests of the electorate": "The chief merit of the principle of participation is to insure that the government respects the rights and welfare of the governed."[27] Democracy ensures the "responsibility" of the governors to the governed. The liberal conception of politics calls for democracy to ensure that leaders are dependent upon the people as their source of power so that they will advance the people's *private* interests.[28]

Democracy, like politics in general, is thus of instrumental value to the liberal, but this value is tenuous at best. Democratic politics requires many conditions which, given the nuisance political activity can be, makes it not always worth the many costs involved. Democracy requires of its citizens time, a certain amount of knowledge or information, and an interest in public affairs, all of which the liberal sees as getting in the way of his or her primary, *private* life. From early on, liberals understood the conditions necessary to self-government. Locke believed that most people did not possess the time and information necessary to take part in political affairs:

> The greatest part of mankind . . . are given up to labour and enslaved to the necessity of their mean condition, whose lives are worn out only in the provisions for living. These men's opportunities for knowledge and inquiry are commonly as narrow as their fortunes, and their understandings are but little instructed, when all their whole time and pains is laid out to still the croaking of their own bellies or the cries of their children. It is not to be expected that a man, who drudges in all his life in a laborious trade, should be more knowing in the variety of things done in the world than a packhorse, who is driven constantly forwards and backwards in a narrow lane and dirty road only to market should be skilled in the geography of the country.[29]

But if early liberals saw the tenuous quality of democracy as a political form, they still supported *in theory* some kind of self-government and political equality. Modern liberals are much more aware of the tenuousness of democracy and, given modern conditions, are much less firmly convinced about even the theoretical desirability of democracy. Modern liberals, like their earlier counterparts, do not see democratic politics as a way of achieving "the common good" or justice, or as a route to self-fulfillment, but are primarily concerned with peace, stability, efficiency, and order in politics. Unlike their predecessors, however, many modern liberals feel that contemporary conditions mean that anything but the most limited democratic participation is deleterious to the primary goals of stability and efficiency. Walter Lippmann feels that at one time in human history political environments were small and isolated enough, and public knowledge was good enough, for self-government to work. He says, however, that modern problems of scale and the lack of both interest and accurate information among citizens make democracy a hindrance to, rather than a facilitator of, good government. Now that "the range of political knowledge [is] limited," Lippmann argues, "the area of self-government would have to be limited."[30]

For these modern liberals, individuals brought together in large masses with little interest in or knowledge about public affairs and with a potential for "irrational" political choice cannot engage in "efficient" political action, and may even threaten the "survival of the total democratic system."[31] Democratic participation must be limited to the occasional choice among "competing elites." Robert Dahl says, "In order for the people to make their choices *effective* on matters of importance to them they will need some stages of government that are less 'democratic' than others."[32] Indeed, among some "liberal democrats" today, apathy and passivity among the citizenry are not considered to be indicators that democracy is malfunctioning, but on the contrary are seen as a positive service to democratic stability and order.[33]

This modern liberal anxiety about the dangers of democracy serves to reinforce the liberal concern about the nature of politics and political solutions. Given the subjective nature of human interests and the primacy of private life, along with the potential for danger that self-government can bring about, liberals feel that the purview of public judgment ought to be limited as far as possible. Most liberals want to keep government out of as many areas as possible, and are very wary of giving it any additional powers beyond those of making and enforcing the most general laws necessary to protect individuals living within the society. For liberals, individual rights and liberties are primary: the political arena is at best a conduit to their pursuit, and at worst an adversary power which threatens to crush their expression.

Despite the liberal concern with minimizing the potentially oppressive aspects of the state, however, the liberal does not retain the independence of the original "state of nature." All liberal preten-

sions about the rights and liberties of the individual aside, the fate of
liberal women and men within the social order may actually be that
of submissive subjects rather than freely acting individuals. Given
the liberal psychology, some kind of public order which can bring
about stability and moderate the devastating effects of individual
conflict is critical. The coercive hand of politics is always necessary
to provide organization and cooperation between individuals and to
facilitate the satisfaction of everybody's interests. According to
writers like Hobbes, the "coercive" political order often requires a
submission which denies individual liberty. Hobbes sees the
sovereign as "a sure and irresistible power [who] confers a right of
dominion and ruling over those who cannot resist."[34]

Hobbes does not represent all liberals, however. Indeed, liberalism is perhaps most clearly defined as a political philosophy which
emphasizes the need to restrain political power. But if politics is
limited in scope, and people are not primarily political animals, no
liberal writer leaves them with the freedom or independence that
they had in their "natural" state. Liberal men and women are not
completely isolated. Locke argues that while desires are subjective
and drive people apart, creating problems in the political process,
there are also human "inclinations" to sociability:

> God having made man such a creature, that, in his own judgment it
> was not good for him to be alone, put him under strong obligations of
> necessity, convenience and *inclination* to drive him into *society*, as
> well as fitted him with language to continue to enjoy it.[35]

But when talking about "society" neither Locke nor more contemporary liberals mean "political society." Locke's society consists of
institutions such as the family, servant/master relationships, and
other social organizations or clubs.[36] Thus the bonds of the liberal
state are social rather than political.

This distinction between the social and the political suggests that
while most liberals limit the scope of politics and refrain from giving
the political order much authority over people's lives, they do not so
limit the scope of society. Although the political order is of much
concern to them, they nevertheless tend to accept the bonds of the
social order as given. For instance, Locke argues that while women
and men resign to the political order the right to impose their will or

rule on others by force, "yet they retain still the power of thinking well or ill, approving or disapproving of the actions of those whom they live amongst and converse with; and by this approbation and dislike they establish amongst themselves what they will call virtue and vice."[37] For Locke, the "approval and disapproval" of social opinion and custom is a much more powerful ruler over people's lives than the political order:

> As to the punishments due from the laws of the commonwealth, they frequently flatter themselves with the hopes of impunity. But no man escapes the punishment of their censure and dislike who offends against the fashion and opinion of the company he keeps and would recommend himself to.[38]

Since "every man strives to accommodate himself to the rest," to "conform himself into one firm and lasting edifice,"[39] the liberal conception finds its love of liberty in as precarious a position in a limited democratic state (due to the "compulsion" from non-governmental sources such as social opinion) as in Hobbes's kingdom.[40]

A coherent picture of democratic politics and the democratic citizen emerges, notwithstanding the ambiguities of the liberal conception of politics and society just discussed. Liberals see human beings as fundamentally apolitical. Political interaction and democracy as a specific form of political interaction are instrumental to the liberal's primary goal of private happiness. Politics can provide the peace and security under which each individual can pursue private interests. The liberal enters the public realm as a free and independent entity with particular personal desires, and the political system allows, nay guarantees, the continuation of his or her particularity and isolation.

The liberal model of the democratic citizen, where it exists at all, is minimalist in nature. The "good citizen" is one who internalizes certain rules and standards of public behavior that are useful in providing for the orderly accommodation of private wishes in the public realm. He or she should know the state's laws, along with the penalties for disobeying them, and thus should understand that it is in both his or her short-term interest (to avoid the immediate punishments) and long-term interest (to avert anarchy) to uphold such laws. "Good citizens" will participate in politics to the extent necessary to provide for their particular interests; they will vote for public officials and legislators who will "represent" them in public affairs, and may from time to time fulfill the duties of public office themselves. But they will not generally participate *directly* in the making of laws or public policy with their fellow citizens. Participation does not define the role of the democratic citizen under the liberal model. Neither will individuals be transformed into "public beings" by their minimal political activity; their character is not altered in political life. The role of "good citizen" is secondary to, if even a part of, what liberals consider being a "good (wo)man."

Political Education: Learning the Lessons of Liberal Citizenship

We have seen that liberals assign only an instrumental role to the artifice of democratic politics. Education also being an artifice of sorts, it follows logically that liberals would be cautious about investing it with a primary role in the development of women and men. The liberal psychology might imply a minimal education which would leave people alone to develop naturally in ways they see fit. On the contrary, however, education is quite important under the liberal conception. Locke felt that the individual is completely dependent upon education for his or her final development: "Of all the men we meet with nine parts of ten are what they are, good or evil, useful or not, by their education. It is that which makes the great difference in mankind."[41]

The liberal believes that nature does not equip us for all the situations or experiences we will face in the world. We enter life with nothing but "a whole world of possibilities, all of them dependent upon eminently artificial discipline for being realized," so that education is the key to our being able to realize our "possibilities."[42] In fact, it is through education that natural instincts which impede individuals either in their development or in their interaction with society can "be modified to any extent, or even conquered."[43]

The empiricist epistemology associated with liberal political thought also dictates a concern with education. Since the individual is a *tabula rasa* to be written on by the environment, his or her entire experience in the world is an "education" which prepares him or her for coping with and overcoming the environment. Education broadly defined is thus the foremost concern of liberal epistemology.

Education is also crucial to our social life. In the liberal understanding of human psychology, men and women are naturally apt to be isolated from one another or at each other's throats in competition for some external good, rather than united in society. Civil society brings the tangible benefits of order and stability, it is true, but only with education can individuals see that the benefits of society outweigh the costs involved. Thus Hobbes could argue that "man is made fit for society not by nature, but by education."[44] Education teaches us that the enjoyment of our natural rights and liberties is made optimal by life in civil society, which carries with it certain obligations and responsibilities to others. Education also can teach us how to make our behavior conform to the legitimate dictates of the social order.

This liberal conception of education *does not* include the direct teaching of politically relevant lessons by the state, however. It is not one of the purposes of politics to educate or cultivate the character of citizens. And given that the role of the citizen is so narrowly defined, liberals see very little educative potential, and great potential for abuse, in political institutions or authorities which try to teach the values or norms of citizenship.

The idea of direct political education of citizens by public institutions is deprecated throughout the liberal tradition. Though Locke sees moral education as a fundamental part of a person's development, nowhere in any of his educational writings do we find a discussion of teaching a child to be a citizen or a participant in politics. All virtues to be learned are private or social, not political. In fact, since "direct virtue" (understood as individual or social virtue) "is the hard and valuable part to be aimed at in education," it is dangerous to entrust this "valuable part" of education to the schools or other political institutions. The lessons of moral education are best learned at home from the father, or with a private tutor, either of whom can "ripen [a child] up sooner into a man, than any at school can do." Locke says that the "principles of justice, generosity, sobriety, joined with observation and industry [are] qualities which I judge schoolboys do not learn much of one another" in public settings or institutions. Locke is quite suspicious of any civic education conducted by public institutions, and does not include any political lessons among his general aims of education.[45]

Mill goes farther than other liberals in establishing a role for the public order in education, since he holds that education is necessary to a citizen's proper (though limited) political participation: "Universal teaching must precede universal enfranchisement."[46] But Mill also denies the polity a *primary* role in citizenship education:

> A general state education is a mere contrivance for molding people to be exactly like one another; and as the mold in which it casts them is that which pleases the predominant power in the government . . . it establishes a despotism over the mind, leading by natural tendency to one over the body. . . . An education established and controlled by the state should only exist, if it exists at all, as one among many competing experiments.[47]

Since one prerequisite to full citizenship, for Mill, is education, the state can enforce educational standards through the establishment of examinations, but only over "instrumental parts of knowledge." Such examinations must be "confined to facts and positive science exclusively"; which means that Mill is unwilling to require any knowledge beyond the "three R's" as necesary to democratic citizenship.[48] In other areas, such as politics, or social and religious values in general, the state may at most test only whether individuals have been made aware of all competing opinions so that they can make up their own minds on these matters: "All attempts by the state to bias the conclusions of its citizens on disputed subjects are evil; but it may very properly offer to ascertain and certify that a person possesses the knowledge requisite to make his conclusions on any given subject worth attending to."[49] Ultimately Mill calls for the reform of private universities as the best method for educating people; politics and political institutions are trivialized as carriers of citizenship education, due to their tendency to "establish a despotism over the mind."

The view that the political order ought to be involved only minimally in the teaching of public values and political lessons is entirely consistent with the minimalist conception of the democratic citizen which liberals maintain. Given that "the role of citizen presupposes so few special qualities,"[50] it is to be expected that liberals would be cautious of the polity's involvement in "moral" or "civic" education. Yet liberals are deeply concerned with the public as well as the private benefits of education. Education is required because, at a minimum, certain rules and standards of public behavior must be taught so as to provide for the orderly accommodation of private wishes in the public realm. The liberal desire for a minimal state depends upon people's ability to rule themselves, which in turn depends upon their education (both formal and informal). The state can be minimized only if individual education is maximized. What, then, is the source of this liberal education, how does it normally take place, and what are its political ramifications?

Under the liberal conception, education usually is put into the hands of the family or society, to be carried out until the young person is able to act autonomously. For Locke, the "education and nourishment" of children is the proper duty of parents, specifically of the father. Locke calls this a "temporary government" where the "ignorance and infirmities of childhood" are "restrained and corrected" by parental education. Children are thereby brought to "a state of knowledge, wherein they may be supposed capable to understand that rule, whether it be the law of nature, or the municipal law of their country they are to govern themselves by," at which point the "business" of education "is over." This "temporary government" of the family which "terminates with the minority of the child" is not given over to public authorities; once majority is reached, the individual is on his or her own.[51] For Locke and Mill, "society" also is involved in this education of the young, through which it enforces its opinions and "its ordinary standard of rational conduct."[52]

Given the liberal psychology, however, even this parental and social education is not an easy task. Students are likely to be pushed and pulled by their passions no matter what their teachers try to do:

Matters that are recommended to our thoughts by any of our passions take possession of our minds with a kind of authority and will not be kept out or dislodged, but, as if the passion that rules were for the time the sheriff of the place and came with all the posse, the understanding is seized and taken with the object it introduces, as if it had a legal right to be alone considered there.[53]

In addition to the fact that the desires are primary rulers within women and men, an education that tries to inculcate socially acceptable behavior is also complicated by the fact that people seek dominion over others. Given the liberal understanding of human psychology, the pupil will be "desirous to be master of [himself] and others,"[54] and will initially balk at lessons on proper social or moral conduct.

John Locke offers a solution to the problem of education, which many liberal educators after him have adopted. First of all, early on, the tendency to dominion in the child and the child's obedience to his own passions alone must be counteracted by establishing the mastery and power of the father. Locke wants to make sure to "establish the authority of a father, as soon as [the child] is capable of submission, and can understand in whose power he is."[55] Only in this way can children be taught to "deny the satisfaction of their own desire."[56] So on one front, the dominion and mastery of the father are used to counteract that very same desire for dominion which is a part of the child's natural psychological makeup.

Locke then moves on to the second front: the nature and content of the education which will develop a child into an orderly social being. Given human psychology as he sees it, Locke understands that some self-interested passion will have to be linked with the lessons of reason in order to overcome the socially devastating effects of accumulated self-interested passions. After discarding "the rod" and "the carrot" as incentives to education, Locke latches on to public "esteem and disgrace" as incentives powerful enough to direct the student's thoughts and behavior:

> Esteem and disgrace are, of all others, the most powerful incentives to the mind, when once it is brought to relish them. If you can once get into children a love of credit, and an apprehension of shame and disgrace, you have put into them the true principle, which will constantly work, and incline them to the right.[57]

The task of the educator, either father or private tutor, is to habituate the student to a "love of praise and commendation," to make him or her "as sensible of credit and shame as may be." If the child can be taught to care about what others think, and to internalize through habit practices consonant with such a concern for public praise and blame, the educator will "have put a principle into him, which will influence his actions, when you are not by; to which the fear of a little smart of a rod is not comparable."[58] In this way the pupil is taught to defer to others and to be obedient to the dictates of the social order, which are necessary to his or her own happiness. And, Locke argues, such an education is squarely in the student's interest, since he or she will be able to gain a more subtle form of power over others through their respect and esteem than the "insolent dominion" acquired through direct mastery of one will over another.[59] By being thus instilled with the habit of obedience to public rules and standards, the child is also taught the proper observance of the rules of the political order, and without the "dangerous" intervention of the political order in such education.

The political implications of this "social education" are serious. The polity is not allowed to get too involved in teaching people to adopt and internalize public values or beliefs, but society can enforce its standards of thought and behavior at will. In fact, given the "soft underbelly" of the liberal psychology—the idea that most men's *social psychology* is so convention-oriented—all government need do is ensure that the social structure and public laws remain cohesive over time; society, through the Law of Opinion and Reputation and an education which will teach obedience to these "laws of private censure," will do the rest to ensure order and stability. Mill argues that the purpose of education is to "train the human being in the habit, and thence the power, of subordinating his personal impulses and aims, to what were considered the ends of society . . . of controlling in himself all feelings which were liable to militate against those ends and encourage all such as tended towards them."[60] By getting an individual into the habit of denying himself in line with society's dictates, obedience to the government's laws could easily be obtained as well, and without involving the government in the teaching of political ends to which the individual ought to "subordinate his personal impulses." Here again, however, the problem of *social* conformity in liberal thought ambiguously rears its head.

Not only does this conception of education bring into question the individual's autonomy in the face of social convention, but it also seems to raise problems for democratic citizenship. Politics is seen as unimportant to education, under the liberal view, and also as a realm which involves little or no conflict or conflict-transformation. Locke and other liberals want to teach civility and the social skills of pleasantness and conformity. They do not want people to be "contradictory or opposing," always making "grave and solid representations" in the public realm.[61] The future citizen should not be brought up in the "art and formality of disputing" since this will produce someone "priding himself in contradicting others, or which is worse, questioning every thing, and thinking there is no such thing as truth to be sought, but only victory, in disputing." Such behavior would be "misbecoming a gentleman."[62]

But the behavior Locke wants to instill in his "gentlemen" appears to be "misbecoming" a democratic citizen, since conflict, debate, and an ultimate resolution of conflict would seem to be an inherent part of democratic, and especially "liberal-democratic," politics. The relationship between teacher and student indicated by such an education also seems undemocratic, since the student is seen as a passive receptacle of social opinions and habits, "something" the teacher brings to "a state of knowledge." This concept of education is a paradox, given the concern with autonomous, consenting individuals which lies at the heart of much of the liberal theory. Liberal education reinforces the duality of the liberal citizen discussed earlier. It befits the person who is either freely pursuing private business or, when relating to the political order, approaching it solely as a passive, obedient *subject.*

In addition, any political teaching done under a liberal conception, either by society or the family, or even the polity, is intended only to teach people the basic rules of the game necessary to peaceful social coexistence, to make people "decent and orderly," respectful of their "lawful superiors."[63] It is not the function of education to transform individuals into "citizens," but to facilitate their existence together as distinct persons.[64] People must be taught to order their behavior in line with certain social rules, but not to transcend their legitimate particularity in order to fit in with a nonexistent "public good." Government may act "in the character of a tutor upon all the members of the state," but its tutorial function consists solely in getting people to "fashion their behavior" in light of the punishment (both overt and covert) they will receive if they go against the laws and customs of society, rather than helping them to internalize a set of common beliefs and goals.[65]

Finally, the empiricist epistemology existing as a foundation for liberal education also has serious political implications. An empiricist outlook makes it difficult to argue for any kind of intersubjective knowledge or values. Since our experience is personal, "public lessons" are hard to legitimate; at most we can resort to "stipulative definitions" about morality which all agree upon as reflective of experience and their perception of it. Empiricist rationalism also tends to deny an *affective* content to education.

Moreover, the empiricism associated with the liberal conception of education implies a lack of knowledge about where empirical knowledge should begin and end. Empiricists can only add up the individual's various educational experiences and put them together into an aggregated whole. Without some view of the whole, however, empiricist educators cannot impose an order or a direction on our education to integrate it in light of social or political purposes. As a result, liberal education tends to be fragmented and undirected, a problem from the standpoint of civic education as we will see later on (Part II, chapter 4).

The liberal model as laid out here may seem rather extreme and no longer applicable to modern democratic societies. But this very conception has been and continues to be the predominant vision in American politics and education. Rush Welter argues that the history of American thought has stemmed from an acceptance of both liberal-democratic politics and a system of popular education which served "as a primary instrument of social order and social organization, the means by which overarching social values and social responsibilities would be enforced."[66] Historically, American thought has contained a prevalent strain which argues for "anarchy with a schoolmaster."[67] Popular education has been seen as "a wise and liberal police" which serves "as well against open violence and overthrow as against the slow but sure undermining of licentiousness."[68] Public education was meant to soften the centrifugal force of a diverse and continually diversifying society by infusing a set of attitudes and behaviors which could provide for social order. It was not seen by most American thinkers as a device to teach common political values (only those norms of the most general sort, such as obedience to law, respect for rights, toleration) or to transform private individuals into public citizens.

Contemporary American writings also reflect the liberal conception of the democratic citizen and of citizenship education. John Gibson, in his article on citizenship education in the *Encyclopedia of Education,* defines the object of citizenship education as being to "convey a body of knowledge . . . considered necessary for the sustenance and well-being of the nation" fitting in with the goals of the polity. But, he continues, "there is no absolute consensus as to what these goals actually are, and probably this is wise in a democratic and diverse society"; thus, the polity does not involve itself in the direct teaching of substantive public values or citizenship norms. What it *does* teach all falls under basically liberal categories:

1   Knowledge of and respect for public law.
2   Development of skills and activities and the acquisition of knowledge necessary for "effective participation" (unspecified).
3   Knowledge and behavior which recognizes and respects the equal rights and opportunities of others.
4   Knowledge and behavior which advance the individual's self-reliance in economic and social life.[69]

Here the political order is seen as a legitimate educator, but one which only minimally educates its citizens to respect the law and the equal rights of others and to participate "effectively" in politics. The role of the citizen seems narrowly defined here, in line with the liberal conception.

In addition, though he moves away from liberal theory in many other respects, John Rawls still adheres to a liberal view of citizenship and political education. Rawls does argue that a "well-ordered society" depends upon its members' acquisition of a "sense of justice" and on a development of "moral attitudes." He also conceives of a developmental psychology which differs from the liberal psychology in that individuals develop "fellow feeling" and "social attachments" over time which then become intrinsic to the self. But in Rawls's discussion, moral development and "moral education" take place through "the approbation and disapprobation of parents and of others in authority . . . who when necessary use rewards and punishments ranging from bestowal and withdrawal of affection to the administration of pleasures and pains."[70] Moral education also takes place through the "praise and blame" of those in society. Through pressure to adopt social roles and through "guilt" placed upon the individual for failing to live up to the demands of social association, society teaches the individual to take up moral attitudes and acquire a "sense of justice." Rawls sees no place for political education, nor in fact does he mention the word "education" when speaking of citizens in the political realm (which goes along with his failure to "define an ideal of citizenship"). Thus Rawls looks very much like Locke or Mill in his depiction of democratic citizens and their proper moral education.[71]

This, then, is the liberal conception of democracy and political education, which itself may be one root of the contemporary educational crisis discussed above. Early liberal thought was predicated upon a homogeneous social and cultural order, where the individualism of the liberal theory of the self could coexist with the demands for order in liberal politics, and where society and the family *could* instill moral norms and common values in their members. This liberal vision of politics and education breaks down under the vast heterogeneity of modern society. In the absence of any fundamental agreement in civil society over values or even the rules of the game, and in the consciously determined absence in liberal thought of a political order which can teach citizens to internalize certain common norms, the danger of the disappearance of any extra-individual order through which people can coexist is real.

Still, the liberal vision seems prevalent in contemporary American democratic thought and practice. And as we will see in Part II, even many of the solutions to the crisis in American education reflect the liberal view, suggesting a lack of faith in any direct democratic political education. An alternative model of democratic politics and civic education is needed, and though the liberal view is prevalent in American thought, there is an alternate vision of the citizen and of civic education which has often existed alongside the liberal model. This is what we will call the "participatory-republican" conception, and it is to this alternative that we now turn.

NOTES

1. In my discussion of both conceptions of democratic politics and citizenship, individual thinkers will be used to illustrate the general arguments of each position. There are certainly differences between each of the thinkers illustrating both the liberal and participatory-republican conceptions, and it is unlikely that any one thinker holds steadfast to all of the notions set out under his or her respective model. But there is a basic continuity and general consistency between the thinkers placed under each conception, and each conception has coherence as an alternate vision of democratic politics and citizenship. We will be concerned primarily with explicating each general model of psychology, politics, and political education, understanding that each is an "ideal-type" which will be used as a heuristic device in exploring contemporary issues in American civic education, and not an iron cage within which to imprison various thinkers who are full of philosophical complexities.

2. Jeremy Bentham, *An Introduction to the Principles of Morals and Legislation*, in *The Utilitarians* (New York: Anchor Books, 1973), 17.

3. Ibid., 100.

4. John Locke, *An Essay Concerning Human Understanding*, ed., John Yolton (London: J. M. Dent and Sons, Ltd. [Everyman's Library]), 27.

5. I have consciously made every effort to adhere to a gender-blind usage in writing this book. This is a difficult task in the field of political theory, a discipline with a long tradition of discourse on "political man," the "good man" and the "good citizen," and "the nature of man." Consequently, there may be passages containing references to "man" or "men" in the writings of the original political theorists, followed by my own gender-neutral statements. In addition, in some instances the requirements of style have been sacrificed somewhat to achieve gender equality. I hope readers will bear with these moments, understanding that in a book about democratic ideals to neglect linguistic traditions which suggest something less than the complete political equality of men and women would be a crime far greater than the few stylistic indiscretions contained here. Special thanks go to Karen Engle for her help in cleaning up the sex biases in the original manuscript.

6. Thomas Hobbes, *Leviathan* (New York: Collier Books, 1962), 62.

7. *The Federalist Papers,* no. 6 (New York: New American Library, 1961), 56.

8. Locke, *Essay,* 262–3, 274.

9. Thomas Hobbes, *DeHomine, Man and Citizen,* ed. Bernard Gert (New York: Anchor Books, 1972), 45–46; Hobbes, *Leviathan,* 53–55.

10. Locke, *Essay,* 208.

11. Locke, *Essay,* 214. Locke also argues that other human emotions or values are ultimately derived from pleasure and pain: "We love, desire, rejoice, and hope only in respect of pleasure; we hate, fear, and grieve only in respect of pain ultimately; in fine, all these passions are moved by things only as they appear to be the causes of pleasure and pain"; *Essay,* 192.

12. John Locke, *Of the Conduct of the Understanding,* ed. Francis Garforth (New York: Teachers College Press, 1966), 36.

13. Roberto Unger, *Knowledge and Politics* (New York: Free Press, 1975), 45.

14. Hobbes, *Leviathan,* 80.

15. John Locke, *Second Treatise of Government,* ed. Peter Laslett (New York: New American Library, 1960), 320.

16. Locke, *Essay,* p. 256.

17. Walter Lippmann, *Public Opinion* (New York: The Free Press, 1922), 110.

18. Bentham, *An Introduction*, 275.

19. Hobbes, *De Cive*, in Gert, *Man and Citizen*, 181.

20. Ibid., 181. A similar statement is found in *Federalist* no 51, 322.

21. *Federalist* no. 10, 78–79.

22. Locke, *Second Treatise*, 395–96.

23. See John Rawls, *A Theory of Justice* (Cambridge, Mass: Harvard University Press, 1971), 554.

24. Locke, *Second Treatise*, 405.

25. Ibid., 405.

26. See for example Hobbes, *De Cive*, 229–30; 111; 232–33. In the American context, see especially *Federalist* no. 49, 315, where Madison strenuously objects to "a frequent reference of constitutional questions to the decision of the whole society" or even "occasional appeals to the people" on the grounds that there is a likelihood of "danger" to "public tranquility" by "interesting too strongly the public passions" in such a way. See also Lippmann, *Public Opinion*, 195–97; Rawls, *Theory of Justice*, 227–28.

27. Rawls, *Theory of Justice*, 230.

28. Representative democracy as conceived by liberal theory seems to exude the same propensity toward domination and mastery as the liberal psychology. The representative is called upon to represent *my* interests in the public realm, and is *my* representative. The "good representative" has no public identity other than that of the discloser of his constituent's interest.

29. Locke, *Essay*, 297.

30. Lippmann, *Public Opinion*, 169.

31. Bernard Berelson, et al., *Voting* (Chicago: University of Chicago Press, 1954), 312.

32. Robert Dahl, *After the Revolution: Authority in a Good Society* (New Haven: Yale University Press, 1970), 93; see also Joseph Schumpeter, *Capitalism, Socialism, and Democracy* (New York: Harper & Row, Publishers, 1950), chap. 22.

33. W. H. Morris Jones argues that political apathy is "a sign of understanding and tolerance of human variety" and contends that it has "a beneficial effect on the tone of political life" since it is a "more or less effective counterforce to the fanatics who constitute the real danger to liberal democracy." Jones, "In Defence of Apathy," quoted in M. I. Finley, *Democracy: Ancient and Modern* (New Brunswick: Rutgers University Press, 1973), 4.

34. Hobbes, *De Cive*, 119.

35. Locke, *Second Treatise*, 361–62. For a similar statement from a modern liberal, see Rawls, *Theory of Justice*, 522–23.

36. Rawls's illustrations of associations containing "shared final ends and common activities" include families, friendships, science, art, and even "game players," but no reference is made to the relationship between citizens in a polity; Ibid., 525.

37. Locke, *Essay*, 297.

38. Ibid., 300–01.

39. Hobbes, *Leviathan*, 237.

40. It may be, as Roberto Unger argues, that "liberal men and women are ultimately in the situation of Schopenhauer's porcupines, who huddle together to protect themselves from the cold, but who, when they come together, wound one another with their spines" Unger, *Knowledge and Politics*, 156.

41. John Locke, *Some Thoughts Concerning Education* (New York: Teachers College Press, 1964), 21.

42. John Stuart Mill, "Nature," in *Nature and the Utility of Religion* (London: Longman's, Green, Reader, and Dwyer, 1969), 46.

43. John Stuart Mill, *A System of Logic, Collected Works;* 8 (Toronto: University of Toronto Press, 1974), 859.

44. Hobbes, *De Cive,* 110.

45. Locke, *Some Thoughts,* 50–54. Robert Horwitz argues that the heirs of Locke's teaching in America were similarly negligent of civic education. "Neither the federalists nor the anti-federalists provided an adequate analysis of the character and place of civic virtue in the American Republic and the need for some form of civic education;" "John Locke and the Preservation of Liberty: A Perennial Problem of Civic Education," in *The Moral Foundations of the American Republic* (University of Virginia Press, 1977), p. 133.

46. Mill, *On Representative Government* (New York: E. P. Dutton, 1972), 280.

47. Mill, *On Liberty* (New York: E. P. Dutton, 1972), 129.

48. Ibid., 130–31. In another place, Mill is willing to extend the list of fields of knowledge which would be "eminently desirable" to the citizen, but even then it only includes history and geography (narrowly understood). Mill, *On Representative Government* 280–81.

49. Mill, *On Liberty,* 130–31. Current attempts in the schools to address "the absence of fixed and firm guidelines for both personal and institutional behavior" through values education (or "values clarification," in the new terminology) are very similar to Mill's proposals. Almost all of these programs aimed at teaching ethics are most concerned about avoiding "religious or political indoctrination," so that students are encouraged to take up an ethical point of view, to discuss various approaches to moral and political dilemmas, and "recognize ethical issues." But it is not the goal of any of these programs to infuse moral or political values or to "change student behavior"—these goals are seen as "occasions for indoctrination." See William J. Bennett, "Getting Ethics," *Commentary* 70, no. 6 (Dec. 1980): 62–65.

50. This is taken from Wilhelm Von Humboldt's *The Limits of State Action,* ed. J. W. Burrow (Cambridge: Cambridge University Press, 1969), 51.

51. Locke, *Second Treatise,* 354–56, 428. Horwitz argues here, in fact, that Locke wanted parents to "assume full responsibility for the education of their children, a program that must be undertaken privately," so that the gentry (the leaders of "public opinion") could be re-educated" away from the corrupting influences of a "public education" conducted by the state or church; see Horwitz, "John Locke," 142–44.

52. Mill, *On Liberty,* 100–01.

53. Locke, *Of the Conduct,* 124–25.

54. Locke, *Some Thoughts,* 28.

55. Ibid., 29.

56. Ibid., 28.

57. Ibid., 36.

58. Ibid., 164–65.

59. Ibid., 82.

60. Mill, *Logic,* 921–922.

61. Locke, *Some Thoughts,* 107.

62. Ibid., 150.

63. Adam Smith, *The Wealth of Nations* (New York: Penguin Books, 1970), 618.

64. Sheldon Wolin argues that men and women in the liberal state resemble billiard balls held together by a frame. They are not "fused" to one another, nor should they be, according to liberals; see Wolin, *Politics and Vision* (Boston: Little, Brown and Co., 1960), 276–77.

65. Bentham, *An Introduction*, VI, xii, 66; III, i, 33.

66. Rush Welter, *Popular Education and Democratic Thought in America* (New York: Columbia University Press, 1962), 3–4.

67. Ibid., 4.

68. Daniel Webster, quoted in Welter, Ibid., 81.

69. John S. Gibson, "Citizenship, Teaching of," *Encyclopedia of Education* 2, 135–38.

70. Rawls, *Theory of Justice*, 458.

71. In addition, Rawls's discussion of the acquisition of a "sense of justice" and of moral development in general is always couched in the rhetoric of the *individual's* interaction with society, social association, and the family. The individual comes to acknowledge reciprocal rights and obligations vis-a-vis these groups. But Rawls does not discuss the teaching of collectivities or citizens, either through political participation or through political education. Moral and civic development is, to him, always a transaction between singular individuals and educational agents.

CHAPTER 2

The Participatory-Republican Conception
of the Democratic Citizen

W E HAVE JUST LAID OUT the liberal conception of democratic politics and citizenship and the corresponding
view of political education which derives from liberal
political theory. The liberal vision lies at the forefront of American
thinking about politics and political education, due to the impact of
liberal thinking on the founding fathers and other politicians since
that era. And, as was discussed above, it may also be one of the roots
of our contemporary educational crisis. However, an alternative
model, the participatory-republican conception, also has strong
roots in the American tradition and may offer the theoretical foundation for solutions to contemporary problems in civic education. In
conjunction with the liberal view, the participatory-republican
model will provide the backdrop for a specific exploration into the
schooling of citizens in America which makes up the heart of this
study.

In coining the hyphenated term "participatory-republican" to
designate this alternative conception of politics and citizenship, an
immediate problem arises. There may be an unavoidable tension
between the "republican" and "participatory" traditions in the history of political thought. Thinkers in the republican tradition have
most often been concerned with the constitution of a body politic,
characterized by a balance of ruling elements (some form of "mixed
constitution"), and by an emphasis on civic virtue and public order.

Republicans have tended to prefer the "rule of law" over the "rule of men," a preference which usually predisposes them to reject participatory democratic politics. While most republicans are adherents of citizen participation (in the broadest sense) in the common life of the polity, they do not unequivocally call for universal participation in day-to-day political decisions or in the making of laws. In fact, many modern republicans such as Tocqueville and Ortega, while they seek to promote small-scale participation in civic activities or associations, are as wary of participatory politics in modern "mass" society as the contemporary liberals discussed above.

Similarly, many thinkers who call for participatory democratic institutions do not share the traditional concerns with constitutionalism or the creation of "civic virtue" that characterize republican thought. The participatory tradition of democratic political discourse may indeed spring more commonly from liberal notions about human psychology and politics than from republican conceptions. In this sense, then, the "participatory-republican" label appears to be a misnomer, a misguided attempt to fuse two disparate traditions and ideals.

There is a sense, however, in which these two traditions are and can be integrated. Many modern participatory democrats have called upon elements in the republican tradition—the conception of the human psyche, the concern for public virtue, and the primacy of civic life—to inform their basic premises about politics. And many thinkers in the republican tradition, such as Machiavelli and Montesquieu, have at times been predisposed to approve of greater citizen participation in political decision-making, even if they have ultimately failed to embrace a fully participatory form of politics. We can see at least glimpses of the fusion of republican with participatory ideals in all of the thinkers to be discussed in conjunction with this alternative conception. Moreover, in the works of Rousseau and Jefferson (as shall be seen below) we find a direct attempt to integrate the republican conception of the psyche and politics with participatory democratic institutions, and a model of civic education which struggles to bring the two ideals together.

The purpose of this chapter, then, is not to develop a conception of democratic politics and citizenship which simply assimilates one tradition of discourse (the republican) into another (the participatory), but rather to explicate a general model of human psychology, democratic politics, and citizen education which inhabits the common ground of each ideal. There is a powerful alternative conception of citizenship to be found in this model, one which has been given credence in the history of American thought and which will help guide us through an exploration of the crucial issues in contemporary citizenship education.

Ultimately, the value of this second model of the democratic citizen will become evident in its application to the discussion of practices in contemporary political education which makes up the bulk of this essay. Because the participatory-republican conception as it will be laid out is both internally coherent and practically powerful as an alternative vision in how we conceive of and educate modern-day democrats, we will construct this chapter as would builders of a desperately needed hospital project on the middle of a fault line: aware of the potentially shaky foundations but proceeding, nonetheless, with the magnitude of our purpose foremost in mind.

The "Balanced Psyche" and the Origins of Republican Sociability

The participatory-republican conception starts with a theory of psychology which incorporates yet goes beyond liberal premises. Adherents to this model would not deny the importance of human desires as motivating forces in men and women. Hegel says, "Passions, private aims, and the satisfaction of selfish desires, are . . . most effective springs of action."[1] Participatory-republicans acknowledge that the "satisfaction of selfish desires" is critical to the health and happiness of the individual psyche. In this they agree with liberals.[2]

Where participatory-republicans disagree is in their notions about the role of reason. In the participatory-republican model, reason is *not* merely the servant of the desires; it is an autonomous faculty with motivational forces of its own. Owing to a "developmental" strain found in many of its ideas about psychology, the participatory-republican model holds that the psychology of pleasure and

pain that lies at the forefront of much of liberal thought is characteristic only of the untrained, uneducated "child"—not reflective of full
human potential. Rousseau clearly makes a case for a developmental
human psychology:

> From our birth we are affected in various ways by the objects sur-
> rounding us. As soon as we have consciousness of our sensations, we
> are disposed to seek or avoid the objects which produce them, *at first*
> *according to whether they are pleasant or unpleasant to us,* then
> according to the conformity or lack of it that we find between us and
> these objects, and *finally according to the judgments we make about*
> *them on the basis of the idea of happiness or of perfection given us by*
> *reason.*[3]

For Rousseau, it is only when reason takes its proper place in the
psyche as an independent and primary guide that a person becomes
fully developed.[4]

For participatory-republicans like Rousseau, then, reason and desire ought to be properly understood as existing intertwined; in the
integrated self, reason and desire are interdependent and com-
plementary:

> The human understanding is greatly indebted to the passions, which,
> it is universally allowed, are also much indebted to the understanding.
> It is by the activity of the passions that our reason is improved, for we
> desire knowledge only because we wish to enjoy; and it is impossible
> to conceive any reason why a person who has neither fears nor desires
> should give himself the trouble of reasoning. The passions, again,
> originate in our wants, and their progress depends on that of our
> knowledge.[5]

The integration of reason and desire does not go on without a
hitch, however. If thinkers in the participatory-republican mode
maintain that reason and desire should properly coexist in the
healthy psyche, they also understand that there is an inherent tension and struggle between the two when it comes to directing human activity. Unlike adherents of liberal psychology, participatory-
republicans like Rousseau believe that reason *can* tell us how to
resolve the conflict between duty and inclination, and can facilitate
an individual's choices in this conflict. But Rousseau agrees with
most liberals in arguing that reason is ultimately feeble in translat-

ing its choice into action: "Reason alone is not active. It sometimes restrains, it arouses rarely, and it has never done anything great."[6] In the face of powerful passions, reason is incapable of directing our activities.

Under the participatory-republican conception, the *will* takes on the status of a crucial moral and psychological faculty which can mediate between the claims of reason and multifarious desires, and thereby can bring about a coherent personality. In a possibly fragmented self, drawn to different actions by different drives, compelled by inner forces as well as outer ones, the will can bring all conflicting elements into harmony. For participatory-republicans, the will is the only thing powerful enough to rule the passions: it can make the voice of reason, which is otherwise faint, be heard and heeded. In sum, the will is seen by participatory-republican thinkers to be at the foundation of the truly cohesive, self-sufficient personality, moderating the conflicting demands of desire and reason.[7]

The participatory-republican notion of human psychology contends that human beings are both rational and passionate, and that the individual psyche—properly ordered through the faculty of the will—is healthy only when reason and desire are integrated appropriately. But what about the relationship between the self and other selves, so crucial to a theory of politics? The liberal model conceived of individuals as being primarily private, self-interested beings. Out of liberal premises is also built a social psychology of power-seeking and domination, due to the individual's need to secure his or her interests in the face of future uncertainties and inevitable conflicts with other interested individuals.

Again, participatory-republicans can be said to begin with and then extend liberal premises. While liberals are correct in their depiction of the self's separation and independence from other selves—we are, after all, distinct material entities, our individual bodies serving to separate us from others; and we also have distinct qualities, needs, and interests—they tend to disregard the fact that we have similarities with others, share ends and purposes, and desire various forms of union with other persons. For participatory-republicans, the psychological truth is that individuals are both independent from and dependent upon other individuals.

Participatory-republicans disagree with the liberal picture of the inherent isolation of individuals, and with the psychology of conflict and struggle for mastery and dominion that emerges from the liberal portrait of the self. Rousseau believes individuals are naturally drawn into conscious association with others and need such contact with their fellows to be fully human:

> So long as [man's] sensibility remains limited to his own individuality, there is nothing moral in his actions. It is only when it begins to extend outside of himself that it takes on, first, the sentiments and, then, the notions of good and evil which truly constitute him as a man and an integral part of his species.[8]

For participatory-republicans, there is a cognitive as well as a moral component to human sociability. Cognitively, the capacity for language makes us both individual and social. The very presence of language, which is one way we express ourselves as autonomous individual selves, makes us also social beings existing consciously for each other. Language allows the individual to communicate in universal symbols with others, and to receive acknowledgment from them in turn. Language symbolizes the unavoidably public nature of the individual self. What makes us human is our ability to take and receive others as the objects of our thought and speech. By contrast, "what is anti-human, the condition of mere animals, consists in keeping within the sphere of feeling pure and simple, and in being able to communicate only by way of feeling states."[9]

The moral aspect of sociability is that each individual needs others to complete his or her identity. Our need for recognition from others requires other equals with whom we mutually engage in relationships which express this reciprocal recognition. Since under this conception "our view of ourselves has to be mediated through the views of others," mutual recognition and communion are necessary to the complete development of the self.[10]

Under the participatory-republican model of the psyche, individuals need to associate with their peers in order to make their lives complete. But in this participatory-republicans are not completely dissimilar from liberals. Liberals admit that individuals have ties to others; nature has given us "inclinations" which "drive [us] into society." As members of families and social organizations, and as friends, individuals come together in cooperative fellowship with one another. While the liberal psychology does tend to see many of these associations as instrumental to the naturally self-interested individual, it still recognizes that "we need one another as partners in ways of life that are engaged in for their own sake."[11]

What really distinguishes the participatory-republican theory of the self is that it maintains that women and men have an inherent need for *political* life. The participatory-republican ideal echoes the words of Aristotle, that "man is a being meant for political association"; human beings are by nature political animals.[12] For while the family and other social associations complete the individual ethically by relating to him or her as an "entire individual," they are still based upon an immediacy and particularity which leaves the individual less than whole, and need to be supplemented. Complete fulfillment of self lies in the life of the political community.[13]

For participatory-republicans, the individual actualizes his or her complete self in political activity. Individuals who have conflicting as well as shared interests, who want things for themselves as well as for their fellow citizens, come together in the political arena to engage in reasoned speech and argument about public issues and in collective activity to resolve them. According to the participatory-republican conception, democratic politics is based upon the belief that "the true self . . . can develop only in a vital relation between the unitary person and the group. That is, the self *is* only in a community—a community as distinguished from a mere society, a mere functional organization"—that is, a political community.[14]

But this discussion is fairly abstract. To say, as the participatory-republican conception does, that the individual has an inherent need to live in a political community is not enough. We need to examine the kind of political life and activity this model entails, what its conception of *democratic* politics specifically looks like, and what the nature and character of the democratic citizen is. This preliminary consideration of the participatory-republican psychology leads us logically to the question of what constitutes a legitimate political order under the participatory-republican conception, just as our discussion of liberal psychology led us to consider the liberal model of politics.

Participatory-Republican Psychology
and the Construction of the "Balanced Polity"

The participatory-republican psychology leaves us with a political dilemma of sorts. As opposed to the liberal conception, the participatory-republican picture of the self depicts political life as intrinsically valuable to the individual. The dilemma lies in the fact that while participatory-republican men and women need the public life of their polity, they are also concerned with their personal needs as individual, autonomous moral agents. Though men and women live together in the political order, they also lead individual lives with legitimate interests of their own. Any common ends pursued in public life must also be expressive of the various ends which each person brings into politics. Sara Shumer, in a recent commentary on Machiavelli, articulates well the dialectical nature of "republican political association":

> Men and women inevitably live together, and also carry on individual lives each with its own integrity. Admittedly, both these facts are not simple achievements, but tasks. They are, in fact, the vocations of being human. . . . A political people is one that accepts as theirs the complicated business of working out a meaningful collective life that does not destroy the conditions for individual integrity.[15]

The problem for participatory-republicans is to combine the freedom to pursue one's interests with the restraint imposed by the community's pursuit of common interests, to combine individual consent with obedience to political authority. According to Rousseau, the ideal solution would be "to find a form of association which will defend and protect with the whole common force the person and goods of each associate, and in which each, while uniting himself with all, may still obey himself alone, and remain as free as before."[16] The participatory-republican theory of politics, like liberal political theory, starts with the presupposition of conflict among contending interests. Given our particular natures, the political community will always experience struggle and contention between diverse individuals and their interests, and a major function of participatory-republican politics is to mediate between the claims of these contending individuals. As with the liberal conception, the participatory-republican conception realizes that without conflict, the very "stuff" of politics would disappear:

> The agreement of all interests is formed by the opposition to that of each. If there were no different interests, the common interest, which would never encounter any obstacle, would scarcely be felt. Everything would run smoothly by itself and politics would cease to be an art.[17]

But for participatory-republicans, the recognition of conflicting interests and their legitimacy is only one element of politics. The other is the belief that we also have common bonds and shared interests as members of a political community. Rousseau maintained that "if the clashing of particular interests made the establishment of societies necessary, the agreement of these very interests made it possible."[18] For liberals, whatever relationship exists between the polity and the people is purely cognitive. The liberal state tells people that, in exchange for a limited government which will not interfere very much in their private lives, they must comply with what laws do exist in order to guarantee and secure their private satisfaction. The individual's long-term self-interest is thus appealed to cognitively, to persuade her or him to abide by the dictates of public laws (with punishment as the ultimate enforcer of his or her affections). Liberals gain behavioral compliance, but do not transform the individual's affective ties.

Rousseau, like other participatory-republicans, argues that though impersonal law is to be preferred to personal authority, laws are ineffective in restraining people's passions and ordering their behavior: "Laws as a rule, being weaker than the passions, restrain men without altering them."[19] Our affective ties with our fellows cause us to "consider the rest and to wish to be considered in turn," form the basis of shared values in a polity, and provide the baseline from which individuals argue out their conflicting positions on public policy.[20]

Herein lies the basis for a major difference between liberal and participatory-republican politics. Liberals, presupposing the irresolubleness of conflicting interests, want political institutions that will protect and secure the individual's interests in the public realm.

In contrast, participatory-republican politics exists to *transform* the individual's particular interests into the general interest of public law, given the underlying commonality which unites citizens. Liberals posit a polity based upon disinterested procedures which individuals can use to pursue their divergent interests. Rawls is a good example here, since his "two principles of justice" are chosen in a hypothetical "original position" by individuals who know nothing specific about themselves or the ends they will pursue. These "principles" in turn establish institutions which will *ensure* the individual's pursuit of particular goals and "heterogeneous human good" in society. In this sense (though liberals begin with a recognition of individual conflict) liberal politics starts from generality and distinterestedness in order to arrive at the satisfaction of particular desires.

Participatory-republicans posit institutions that begin with individuals who have diverse particular interests and a clear awareness of themselves and their unique situations, but who also have strong social attachments to their fellows. Political institutions and procedures are set up with the formulation of general rules and common norms out of such contending interests in mind. The participatory-republican theory of politics starts with particular divisions before arriving at the public unity, albeit a unity which embodies the individual's particular desires.[21]

In fact, this model would argue that a meaningful political life is only to be had when such a transformation of private into public interests takes place. Adherents to a participatory-republican ideal would be very critical of the liberal notion that politics is a place where individuals come together with their characters already formed and in which the integrity of those previously formed characters is protected and secured. Hegel argues that the political community is a place of ongoing transformation and education of its members, a "community of conscious life" where interests and psyches become "fused," rather than an aggregation of particular interests who contract with the state in order to "maintain [their] particular ends."[22]

Under the participatory-republican conception, the political process is meant to produce "a spirit of the common life . . . which is superior to the opinions of any particular individual because it is the product of diverse experiences and interests."[23] As such, the key element to republican politics is widespread community participation in debates over public issues. The process of public discussion and mutual persuasion is extremely important, since through it citizens express their attitudes, change them and develop new ones, influence political judgment and action, and provoke further problem-solving thought and discussion. It is through a process of public discussion that individuals are transformed in the ways mentioned above: they are led outside themselves and moved to a place beyond where they began, and are thereby able to see their interests in a wider perspective. Roberto Unger feels that participation in political debate is crucial, both for the individual and for the polity as a whole:

> It is only through communication in society that individuals can be developed and revealed. Moreover, the species nature in which all individuals participate is hidden. To discover it and to express it in common purposes of social life, men must be able to compare their individual views and discuss the grounds for those views.[24]

This examination of the importance of public participation in political debate leads us into the question of the nature of *democracy* under the participatory-republican ideal. The liberal conception, as was shown in the preceding chapter, sees democracy as of instrumental value. For liberals, democratic political institutions are required only to ensure that individuals and their interests are equally considered and protected in the public realm. Democracy ensures the responsibility of governors to the needs and interests of the individuals they govern. But since democracy is only of instrumental worth to liberal thinkers, and given the tenuousness of democracy under modern conditions, most liberals are willing to forego anything approaching direct democracy in order to promote efficiency and convenience. Democracy is limited to the selection of those in authority who will *represent* us in the public realm.

Participatory-republicans argue that to conceive of democratic politics in such a way is not only to deny what they think is an essential feature of the complete development of the self, but also to yield the right to equal protection that liberals are so concerned about. A concept of democracy which involves only minimal participation in the selection of those who represent us abandons the hope that individuals can effectively make decisions about the things that affect their lives and interests. Carole Pateman contends that rather than being representative of their rights and needs, liberal democracy actually involves "the alienation by citizens, through elections, of their right to make political decisions." By giving up their power to directly "make political decisions," liberal women and men also relinquish their right to equal protection and security of the ends they wish to pursue.[25]

So, from the standpoint of efficiency and effectiveness, participatory-republicans call for a democratic politics in which citizens participate maximally in collective decisions. Only when each citizen has a "responsible share" in "forming and directing the activities of the groups to which he belongs" can he or she ensure that his or her needs and interests are being heeded and incorporated into the laws and policies of the government.[26]

Moreover, most participatory-republicans would argue that— legitimacy and equal right to protection of interests aside—the people as a whole are better judges of the proper course for the political community than its representatives or selected "experts." Rousseau and Jefferson were adamant about the ability of any and every person to decide on questions of general law. For Rousseau, "the public is the truest judge of morals, and is of such integrity and penetration on this head, that although it may be sometimes deceived, it can never be corrupted."[27] Jefferson went so far as to argue that the "ploughman" was the better judge of morality than the philosopher: "State a moral case to a ploughman and a philosopher. The former will decide it as well, and often better than the latter, because he has not been led astray by artificial rules."[28]

Participatory-republicans not only see a more participatory democratic politics as necessary to the pursuit and protection of individual interests that liberals are concerned about, but also as an essential requirement of human life. Besides being of instrumental value to participatory-republicans, democracy is intrinsically necessary to bring about the fullest self-expression of individual citizens through participation in the affairs of their community. Participatory democracy satisfies the dual nature of the self as conceived in a participatory-republican psychology, since only under such a political association where citizens participate in the making of laws they obey are individuals both independent and dependent, rulers and ruled, free and yet obedient to a higher authority. A participatory democracy is one in which individuals mutually recognize each other as independent agents and accept each other's claims as legitimate, but also recognize their need for communion and political association with each other. A democratic community sees its members as equal partners who mutually contend and reciprocally persuade each other in the process of public deliberation, decision, and action.

Furthermore, the participatory-republican conception of democratic politics can be said to extend liberal epistemology. Modern participatory-republicans agree with liberals about the fact that there may be no "universal truth" on which to ground collective action, yet they also acknowledge a need to act, regardless of this epistemological uncertainty. Democracy reconciles in the public realm the need to act with the absence of universal grounding, as the political community engages in the collective search for public criteria which can direct political activity.[29]

I have just outlined the purpose and character of democratic politics under the participatory-republican conception. However, most thinkers associated with this model would acknowledge that for such an ideal to be realized in practice, certain conditions need to be met which are quite problematic in modern times. First of all, the process of discussion and deliberation among the community's members, which lies at the heart of participatory-republican democracy, requires a political community of limited size, one conducive to face-to-face contact and maximum participation. Rousseau felt that a small political body, "where the people can readily be got together and where each citizen can with ease know the rest,"[30] is important since the ability to share opinions, information, and experiences in face-to-face contact makes it easier for people to discuss and understand public issues and to "achieve a genuine common interest." Power and status are also likely to be better equalized in a small association.[31]

In addition, the kind of fellow feeling and affective bonds that participatory-republican politics depends on demand restrictions on the size of the polity. Beyond a certain physical scale, the relationship between the self and the political community required by this model's politics becomes hard to feel "as a matter of heart."[32] Need-less to say, participatory-republican requirements of scale are nearly impossible to achieve in modern democracies, and any attempt to create smaller political entities through decentralization, even if possible, runs into its own difficulties.[33]

Another important condition for participatory-republican democ-racy is the presence of a great degree of social and economic equal-ity in the political community. The success of Rousseau's *Social Contract* depends upon "a large measure of equality in rank and fortune, without which equality of rights and authority cannot long subsist."[34] If such equality does not exist, the political values shared and the decisions made by the members of the polity are likely to be the outcomes of social and economic determinants which affect some more than others. Dominant factions with greater resources are able to "capture" the public arena and dictate public policy.

These conditions notwithstanding, the ideal of participatory-republican politics is still adhered to by many contemporary polit-ical thinkers. Unlike liberals, who seem willing to forego democracy at the appearance of any problem, participatory-republicans believe that though "a genuinely political society, in which discussion and debate are an essential technique, is a society full of risks," demo-cratic politics understood "as a continued effort in mass education" is a better way of preserving liberty and happiness than public apathy and the abandonment of citizenship by the masses of people.[35] They understand, as did Rousseau, that although the "body politic" may inevitably decay, it is necessary to constitute the most virtuous in-stitutions and sturdiest democratic processes so as "to prolong as much as possible the life of the state."[36]

Here, many contemporary liberals would contend that a major flaw in the participatory-republican theory of politics is that it has an inadequate concept of leadership. In their overriding concern with forging a notion of political authority based directly in the people themselves and in reconceptualizing political obligation as a hori-zontal relationship between citizens and the state, republicans ne-glect the vital need for political leadership, liberals might argue, especially in modern "mass society" which fails to meet the condi-tions under which the "classical" model of participatory democracy was conceived.

However, participatory-republican thinkers *do* have a developed notion of democratic leadership. The role of the participatory-republican leader is outlined in Jefferson's "Letter to John Adams," where he discusses what he calls the "natural aristocracy." As opposed to the "artificial (or pseudo) aristocracy" based upon birth or wealth, the grounds of this natural aristocracy's ability to lead the polity would be "virtue and wisdom." But this natural aristocracy was not a surrogate for active citizen participation—in fact, it was both the necessary condition for and the result of such participation. An active polity, provided with a political education to "raise the mass of the people to the high ground of moral respectability necessary to their own safety and to orderly government,"[37] endowed with relative political and economic equality, and organized into smaller political units (wards) more conducive to meaningful public debate and participation, would be the best qualified to elect "the really good and wise" leaders who in turn would encourage better participation.[38]

As we see from Jefferson's writings, the participatory-republican notion of democratic leadership is integrally connected to a notion of citizenship or "followership"—there is a dialectical relationship between leaders and followers pursuing common purposes in a democratic society:

> Leadership is not a surrogate for participation in a democracy, it is its necessary condition. Without leaders, a citizenry is unlikely to remain active; without active citizens, responsive leaders are unlikely to emerge, and leaders who do emerge are unlikely to remain responsive.[39]

In fact, it may be that liberals, too often concerned with power, fail to see the *relational* nature of democratic leadership. James MacGregor Burns says that true leadership "mobilizes" and engages citizens to realize goals common to both leaders and followers (in a setting of mutual interaction), whereas the "naked power" of liberal theorists merely "coerces" behavior. Following Aristotle, participatory-republicans understand that democratic leadership implies leaders who know how to be ruled as well as rule, to lead and be led—people are transformed from simply followers and leaders into "follower-leaders" and "leader-followers."[40]

I have just sketched the participatory-republican conception of democratic politics. While the liberal conception presents persons as fundamentally apolitical, the participatory-republican model holds that people need political association. Under the participatory-republican conception, citizens share common norms and values and yet treat each other as individual agents deserving equal respect. They come together in face-to-face association to deliberate over issues requiring public action. The government is not just minimally involved in people's lives, extracting "mere obedience" to its laws in order to provide a baseline for individuals to pursue their interests in private; rather, the political community exists to transform individuals and their interests into a public will.

The participatory-republican model of the democratic citizen also differs from its liberal counterpart. Citizenship is not understood here as a minimal duty which involves following certain rules of behavior and voting for those who will represent individuals in the public arena. According to the participatory-republican ideal, citizens have strong ties to their political community, and share common concerns with their fellow citizens. The participatory-republican citizen is understood as "a man who shares in the administration of justice and in the holding of office,"[41] and is thus, following Jefferson's characterization, "a participator in the government of affairs."[42] Citizens discuss, decide, and act together to make public policy, and through such direct participation in politics, their individual character is altered: their purview is expanded, their private interest is changed into the law of the polity, and their personality is made more complete. Since participatory-republicans would contend that to be fully human means to be a member of a political community, to be a good person under their definition, one must also be a good citizen.

Participatory-Republican Political Education: Answering the Question of Balance

The participatory-republican conception holds a participatory democratic politics to be essential both to the effective satisfaction of individual interests and to a complete human life. This model imagines diverse people coming together to share and discuss issues of public impact, working together to search for the common ground of ultimate public decisions and actions. As such, the participatory-republican political project requires certain traits and skills which are not a part of unaided natural human endowment, and must be learned. Jefferson once said, "The qualifications for self-government are not innate. They are the result of habit and long training."[43] In fact, thinkers such as Rousseau and Dewey argue that the entire environment surrounding a person educates him or her, and that without consciously designed educational environments to develop the desirable attributes of citizenship, we would have "chance" environments (or debilitating ones) educating women and men. Without a systematic civic education, the participatory-republican ideal of political life would be stillborn: "What nutrition and reproduction are to physiological life, education is to social life."[44]

A proper political education is crucial to the participatory-republican model of democracy. Dewey argues that a model which "repudiates the principle of external authority,"[45] putting authority instead in the people themselves, must be able to teach people to be self-governing. In order to make people capable of becoming active, equal participants in the affairs of their community, their capacities to do so must be set to work: citizens, through civic education, must be "made worthy of liberty and capable of bearing it."[46] Participatory-republicans understand that there is a real danger in divorcing the powers which they place in the hands of the people from the knowledge necessary to the exercise of these powers. Horace Mann stated:

> If republican institutions do wake up unexampled energies in the whole mass of a people, and give them implements of unexampled power wherewith to work out their will; then these same institutions ought also to confer upon that people unexampled wisdom and rectitude. . . . If we maintain institutions, which bring us within the action of new and unheard-of powers, without taking any corresponding measures for the government of those powers, we shall perish by the very instruments prepared for our happiness.[47]

One major function of political education under the participatory-republican model, then, is to teach people the art of self-governance. But Dewey believes education is also required because of the kind of political life envisioned under a participatory-republican democracy:

> A democracy is more than a form of government—it is primarily a mode of associated living, of conjoint communicated experience. The extension in space of the number of individuals who participate in an interest so that each has to refer his own action to that of others, and to consider the action of others to give point and direction to his own, this widening of the area of shared concerns . . . is a matter of deliberate effort to sustain and extend.[48]

Civic education helps bring to people the experience and joy of shared concerns and interests, and teaches the citizen the need to be able to "refer his own action to that of others." Since they see democracy as the "realization of a form of social life in which interests are mutually penetrating," participatory-republicans want the political community to engage in a "deliberate and systematic education" which can inculcate public harmony and other-regardingness.[49]

These arguments make the case for the *social* benefits of a proper political education. But if participatory-republicans believe that the public education of citizens is necessary to the optimal functioning of the polity, they also agree with liberals that education is crucial to the development of individual character. According to Rousseau, individuals need education to insure their proper intellectual and psychic growth:

> We are born weak, we need strength; we are born totally unprovided, we need aid; we are born stupid, we need judgment. Everything we do not have at our birth and which we need when we are grown is given us by education.[50]

Given the dual nature of the human psyche under the participatory-republican conception, education becomes critical to individual moral development. As Rousseau understands it, reason and conscience are vital elements in the self, but they are "timid" in the face of "the noise" of "prejudices" and passiions, and must be brought out through education. Emile asks his tutor to "make me free by protecting me against those of my passions which do violence to me. Prevent me from being their slave; force me to be my own master and to obey not my sense but my reason."[51] But the tutor knows that this is no easy task. He understands that reason alone is ineffective in commanding the passions; he realizes that "one has a hold on the passions only by means of the passions. It is by their empire that their tyranny must be combated."[52] As we saw above, the faculty of the will does exist to mediate between reason and desire. Under the participatory-republican psychology, the will *is* strong enough to rule the passions. But given a possibly fragmented self, the will must be properly educated.

Education can give the will the strength and the "erotic energies" necessary to put it in control over the contending elements within the psyche; education can liberate such "erotic impulses" and put them on the side of virtue and reason. Since the will is properly understood by participatory-republicans as the mediator between reason and desire, and since most terms which denote character "denote various ways in which men *willfully* relate their thought to their existence,"[53] political education is essential in the development of character through the strengthening of the will. Furthermore, according to Rousseau, a proper education can develop feelings of autonomous self-love *(amour d'soi)* while avoiding the full emergence of self-love which is totally dependent upon others *(amour propre)*. With the right education, an individual can get his or her faculties in balance and thus lead a better life.[54]

But why must this education be a political education? Liberal thinkers regard moral education as properly taking place *away from* the political community or its institutions. Since, under the liberal conception, the political lessons one needs to learn are minimal, the valuable part of such education—individual moral instruction—is to be conducted by the private family in conjunction with the society around the child.

Participatory-republicans would on the whole reject the fundamental tenets of this liberal idea of education, as many of its allegedly nonpolitical teachings have serious political messages and implications which contradict their conception of democratic citizenship. First of all, in contrast to liberal theory, the participatory-republican conception of politics presupposes many qualities in its citizens which must be taught. And given the tension in republican thought between the polity and family discussed earlier, particpatory-republicans would argue that the family cannot possibly teach civic norms and values. The family will always limit the citizen's purview and divide his or her loyalties.

Moreover, participatory-republicans would argue that the education liberals propose teaches lessons contrary to the true picture of the human self. For Locke, education involves bringing the private passions of praise and blame to bear on the *will* of the child, thus weakening the will and making it serve these destructive passions rather than strengthening it as an ethical mediator within the psyche. The pedagogical use of social praise and blame as proposed by liberal educators produces people who are, to participatory-republican eyes, inauthentic and completely self-regarding. For Rousseau, this "social education" "is fit only for making double men, always appearing to relate everything to others and never relating anything except to themselves alone."[55] According to Rousseau, the liberal education which alerts us only to a concern with reputation and fails to mold the citizen incontrovertibly corrupts people rather than uplifting them. Under such a theory of education,

> nobody troubles himself whether citizens exist or not, and still less does anybody think of attending to the matter soon enough to make them. It is too late to change our natural inclinations, when they have taken their course, and egoism is confirmed by habit: and it is too late to lead us out of ourselves when once the human ego, concentrated in our hearts, has acquired that contemptible activity which absorbs all virtue and constitutes the life and being of little minds.[56]

The participatory-republican ideal maintains, then, that only a publicly conducted civic education can avoid the pitfalls of the liberal method and properly mold individuals who are both complete persons *and* citizens. Only an education characterized by constant public activities and exercises involving dialogue and mutual learning can strengthen the public self against the individual self and thereby educate the whole self (as the participatory-republican psychology conceives of it). An education conducted amongst one's fellows can develop men and women who are autonomous and yet recognize their dependence on others, and can make them fit for egalitarian social relations. In addition, following Aristotle, civic education is best undertaken by the political community since not only does the student receive the proper nurture and instruction when young, but the political community then provides the environment within which to practice the virtues he or she is learning. Since most republicans would agree with Aristotle that a knowledge of virtue without the practice of it is worthless, the political community becomes the ideal educational agent.[57]

We have seen that, for all the reasons cited above, participatory-republicans would agree with Rousseau, who said that a proper civic education "is certainly the most important business of the state."[58] But of what exactly does this education consist? What are the general values, practices, and skills that participatory-republicans want their citizens to learn, and how are they best taught these lessons?

The first lessons of education under the participatory-republican model are directed at developing the proper psychological balance within the individual child. For Dewey, a democratic education is meant "to prepare [the child] for the future life: to give him command of himself; it means to train him that he will have the full and ready use of all his capacities."[59]In order to give the child true "command" and prepare him or her for a "future life" of participatory-republican social relations, Rousseau maintains that early teachings must move children away from the pernicious psychology of "mastery and slavery." Without a proper educational environment early on, children may become accustomed to getting their way in all things, making others submit to their whims, or else others may make them always submit to theirs. In both cases, the pupil learns either "to give orders or receive them. Thus his first ideas are those of domination and servitude. Before knowing how to speak, he commands; before being able to act, he obeys." For Rousseau, the child who develops in such a way is more likely to have a "monarchical" rather than a democratic psychology.[60]

A careful education, however—one that teaches children how to be humble and realistic, how to accept human suffering and defeat, and to know what they can do by themselves and what they are dependent upon others for—can divert young students from "seeking [their] pleasures in dominion and in another's unhappiness." Such an education will develop a person who has "neither the crawling and servile submission of a slave nor the imperious accent of a master," but one with a "modest confidence in his fellow man" and "the noble and touching gentleness of a free but sensitive and weak being who implores the assistance of a being who is free but strong and beneficent."[61] This kind of education befits the potential citizen, under the participatory-republican conception.

Another important aspect of this "psychological education" is the development of a balance between the rational and passionate elements within the self. There must be an affective as well as a cognitive content to participatory-republican education, just as there is an affective and a cognitive element to the model's political component. This recognition of the need for such a "dual education" has important ramifications for, and may raise serious tensions in, educational practices (see Part II, chapter 7).

A more general substance to political education also exists under the participatory-republican conception. Participatory-republicans would acknowledge that students will and should learn things by working alone: by working independently students can learn the autonomy and confidence in themselves that they will need as democratic citizens. But Dewey also believes that "right character is not to be formed by merely individual percept, example, or exhortation, but rather by the influence of a certain form of institutional or community life upon the individual, and that the social organism through the school, as its organ, may determine ethical results."[62] Dewey argues that through the right kind of interpersonal communication between students and teachers, shared ends essential to participatory-republican politics can be developed.[63]

We saw earlier that the liberal conception of political education does not include the idea that citizens should learn to feel common bonds with one another or that they should love their political community. Locke's method of education teaches people only to value others' esteem in order to enhance their self-interest, not to care for others as fellow citizens. Rather than teaching social or public virtue, liberal political education teaches greater privatism, since all other-directedness is grounded in private profit.

Under the participatory-republican model, however, an education which communicates experiences and values to be internalized and shared by all is extremely important, since common bonds between citizens are the primary foundation of a participatory democratic politics. What binds citizens together is the fact that they have common interests, share a common perception of "good and evil, of the just and the unjust, and of similar qualities," and that they share "association" in a common "way of life" grounded in these common perceptions.[64] For participatory-republicans like Rousseau, the proper civic education can make people internalize "the practice of those virtues which they make themselves follow in learning to know them" such as coming to "respect the sacred bonds of their respective communities; [to] love their fellow citizens and serve them with all their might; [and to] scrupulously obey the laws, and all those who make or administer them."[65]

Under the particpatory-republican conception, then, political education is a duty which is extremely important to the political community. Not only must future citizens be instructed in the skills and procedures of self-government, but they must also acquire the affective ties, the belief in common ends, and the psychological predispositions necessary to participate in political life. It is easy to see why Rousseau felt that the task of educating women and men is more important and more difficult than that of governing them.[66] Indeed, proper citizenship education seems to be yet another of the conditions upon which a healthy participatory-republican politics perilously hangs.

But if the participatory-republican model of democratic politics depends upon a structured educational process, it is also true that thinkers like Dewey see democratic politics itself as largely educational:

> Popular government is educative as other modes of political regulation are not. It forces a recognition that there are common interests, even though the recognition of what they are is confused; and the need it enforces of discussion and publicity brings about some clarification of what they are.[67]

A participatory democratic politics brings people into the public forum to discuss and resolve common conflicts and problems, and in so doing teaches each citizen the importance of taking into account wider interests than his or her own. Political participation draws out the citizen's "public self," as he or she is forced to seek compromises and solutions which will also satisfy his or her fellow citizens and their equally legitimate concerns. In the course of actually making the laws and policies under which the community lives, along with others who have distinct interests, citizens learn that equality and justice rather than personal desire are the proper standards of public law.

Moreover, citizens under a participatory-republican politics continually learn more about themselves, their relationship to others and the community at large, and the stake they have in it. They learn to distinguish between their desires and motivations, and begin to define their collective "self" and its judgment on public affairs. Individuals come to know the political facts and conditions surrounding their life's choices, and thereby re-postulate their own interests and choices in a way that they otherwise could not have done.[68]

For thinkers in the participatory-republican mode, citizens who participate in democratic politics take full responsibility for their lives, as they not only have a better understanding of themselves and their relations to others but are able to *act* in conjunction with others to realize their public choices. And for people like Dewey, Hegel, and Rousseau, holders of a somewhat "activist epistemology," political participation also brings knowledge, since knowledge is only had by "acting upon the world." In order to know, according to Dewey, "men have to *do* something; they have to alter conditions."[69] In these ways, then, participatory-republicans see political life as they understand it to be an intrinsically educative and self-developing activity. On this issue John Stuart Mill, who has been otherwise identified with the liberal conception, would agree with the participatory-republican ideal, though other liberals might see the "educative" functions of political participation in mass society as dangerously indoctrinative and a threat to individual freedom.

As we can see, the participatory-republican conception stands in stark contrast to the liberal model, especially regarding the question of civic education. Where the liberal conception sees the role of politics in our lives as minimal and instrumental, and therefore minimizes the functions of overt civic education, preferring instead a private moral education (which, however, has serious political implications), the participatory-republican view holds politics to be an intrinsic part of an individual's life, and requires a "transformational" civic education in line with this view.

Of course, these two conceptions are somewhat oversimplified, and are primarily meant to serve heuristic purposes for the explorations into educational practices which follow. These are not *merely* theories or models, however: they also have great cogency in the history of American politics and education. As we have seen, the liberal conception as laid out has tended to be the predominant American vision. But ideas and institutions of a participatory-republican orientation have also made their way to the forefront of American theory and practice over the years.[70] If the history of American thought has encompassed Hamilton and Madison, it has also included Jefferson; if we have been influenced by Sumner, we have also been influenced by Mann, Bancroft, and Elliot; if the twentieth century has produced John Rawls and Robert Nozick, it has also given us John Dewey.

Another look at Thomas Jefferson's writings should help illustrate the importance in the history of American thought of ideas reflecting the participatory-republican model. From our nation's beginning, Jefferson argued that Americans ought to have freedoms not enjoyed by their English brethren. They ought to enjoy the right to "public happiness," which for Jefferson consists of citizen access to the political arena, the right to be "a participator in the government of affairs."[71] And Jefferson made proposals for Virginia which attempted to accomplish this. Since he believed that "governments are republican only in proportion as they embody the will of their people and execute it," Jefferson demanded "the subdivision of the counties into wards," "small republics" in which "every man in the state" would become "an acting member of the common government, transacting in person a great portion of its rights and duties." Jefferson called the New England townships, upon which his ward proposal was based, "the wisest invention ever devised by the wit of man for the perfect exercise of self-government," as it was only through the direct participation of citizens that "the voice of the whole people would be thus fairly, fully, and peaceably expressed, discussed, and decided by the common reason of society."[72]

Given his conception of democratic politics, Jefferson felt that political education was crucial to bringing about a republican political life: "I know no safe depository of the ultimate powers of the society but the people themselves; and if we think them not enlightened enough to exercise their control with a wholesome discretion, the remedy is not to take it from them, but to inform their discretion by education."[73] It was the political community's responsibility to establish and maintain "a system of general instruction which shall reach every description of our citizens, from the richest to the poor-est,"[74] in order to teach the skills and values necessary to a participa-tory-republican politics. In addition, a system of wards in which all participated politically would be an important educational agent, since "making every citizen an acting member of the government" would initiate them into the practice of public reasoning, persua-sion, and decision-making, giving them all the skills necessary to such deliberation. The wards would also provide the citizen with a lesson in affective bonding by "attach[ing] him by his strongest feelings to the independence of his country, and its republican con-stitution."[75] Jefferson's view of politics and political education as laid out here epitomizes the participatory-republican conception as it has existed alongside the liberal tradition in American thought.

This long discussion of Jefferson is meant to show the strength of this participatory-republican ideal in American political thinking, a strength which has been carried down to contemporary writers. This model may be a reasonable alternative in helping direct our education of citizens, just as Jefferson felt it was at America's found-ing. In the midst of the disarray in which our political and educa-tional institutions now find themselves, the participatory-republican model may be able to offer suggestions for our educational practices as they impact upon the training of citizens. We must now explore the contemporary wisdom and practices in civic education in light of our two models, especially the participatory-republican one, with the education of the *truly* democratic citizen in mind.

NOTES

1. G. W. F. Hegel, *The Philosophy of History* (New York: Dover Press, 1956), 20. Hegel will be considered a republican here, mainly due to the implications of his psychology in *Phenomenology of Mind* and in some of his notions about politics. There are many elements of liberal thought in Hegel's writings, however, and am-biguities in Hegel will be noted throughout the chapter.

2. Desires are not seen an unidirectional, however. Participatory-republicans like Rousseau see that desires can pull us in many directions, and can serve to fragment our purposes and personalities. Liberals tend to see human desires as "vector-like," sending the self out in one direction. For Rousseau, the passions in man can be directed to good or bad. See, for example, Rousseau, *Emile*, 213–14.

3. Ibid., 39, emphasis added.

4. Jean-Jacques Rousseau, *The Social Contract and Discourses*, ed. G. D. H. Cole (New York: E. P. Dutton and Co., 1950), 18–19.

5. Rousseau, "Discourse on the Origins of Inequality," in Ibid., 210. This is also the message of Jefferson's famous dialogue between his head and his heart in letter to Maria Cosway, in *The Portable Jefferson*, ed. Merrill Peterson (New York: The Viking Press, 1975), 400–412.

6. Rousseau, *Emile*, 321.

7. Rousseau and Hegel are the most emphatic about the importance of the will in the human psyche. For Rousseau, not only does the will mediate between passions and reason, "giving each its due," but it also must attempt to "diminish the excess of the desires over the faculties" and thus get our desires and our power to satisfy them in accord with each other. Without this, individuals will end up being miserable; see *Emile*, 80–81. Hegel sees the will as the mediator, through conscious reflection, between the "immediacy of instinctive desire" and "the universality of [rational] thought." See G. W. F. Hegel, *Philosophy of Right*, ed. T. M. Knox (Oxford: Oxford University Press, 1952), 17–22.

8. Rousseau, *Emile*, 219–20.

9. G. W. F. Hegel, *Phenomenology of Mind*, ed. J. B. Baillie (New York: Harper & Row, 1967), 127.

10. Unger, *Knowledge and Politics*, 216.

11. Locke, *Second Treatise*, 361–62; Rawls, *Theory of Justice*, 522–23.

12. Aristotle, *Politics*, ed. Ernest Barker (London: Oxford University Press, 1958), 5.

13. For many participatory-republicans, the family and the polity are in tension. The family exists as both an example of shared purposes and community which takes the individual outside of her or himself, and as a threat to such a community of shared purposes on a larger scale. As such, the family is a source of conflicting loyalties: "The modern family forever draws men back into an association that competes with loyalties to all other groups and offers a measure of individual recognition through love, even in the absence of shared values. So communitarian politics must treat the family as both a source of inspiration and a foe to be contained and transformed"; Unger, *Knowledge and Politics*, 264.

14. Robert Penn Warren, *Democracy and Poetry* (Cambridge: Harvard University Press, 1975), 25.

15. Sara Shumer, "Machiavelli: Republican Politics and Its Corruption," *Political Theory* 7, no. 1 (1979): 13.

16. Rousseau, *Social Contract*, 13–14.

17. Rousseau, *Social Contract*, 27. Richard Sennett has even argued that the transformation of the idea of community, from the notion of community as the union of shared action and shared goals (a sense of "collective self") into that of "collective personality" in the nineteenth-century is a change that reflects the loss of the idea of community as a union of different individuals with conflicting personalities, goals, and interests—whose very conflict produces a harmony in their collective action. For Sennett, the modern notion of *gemeinschaft* is built on the fantasy that all individuals

within the community share the same "motivational structures" and "have the same impulse life," the same personality. This goes against the tradition of republican political theory. See Sennett, *The Fall of Public Man* (New York: Alfred A. Knopf, 1977), 221–23, 238–39, 310–11.

18. Rousseau, *Social Contract,* 23.

19. Rousseau, *Discourse on the Origins,* 263–65.

20. Ibid., 241.

21. Jane Mansbridge differentiates between "adversary" and "unitary" democracy on the basis of whether interests are conflicting (adversary) or basically consensual (unitary). An adversary democracy calls for "each individual to be present, in some sense to protect his or interests at the moment of decision." Unitary democracy has each member participating as a commitment to the common good in a politics of friendship. The problem with Mansbridge's categories, however, is that she has no notion of democratic politics *transforming* conflictual interests into a "common good," given an underlying sense of community. Her "unitary" democracy leaves out much of the meat of politics, the discussion and debate among contending citizens over public issues and their resolution. See Jane Mansbridge, *Beyond Adversary Democracy* (New York: Basic Books, 1980).

22. Hegel, *Philosophy of Right,* 189. This is a major thrust of Benjamin Barber's argument in *Strong Democracy: Participatory Politics for a New Age* (Berkeley: University of California Press, 1984).

23. Dennis Thompson, *The Democratic Citizen* (Cambridge University Press, 1970), 99.

24. Unger, *Knowledge and Politics,* 280. See also Barber, *Strong Democracy,* 173–198, for an extended discussion of the goals and functions of "strong democratic talk."

25. Carole Pateman, *The Problem of Political Obligation: A Critical Analysis of Liberal Theory* (New York: John Wiley and Sons, 1979), 174. Rousseau makes a similar argument about parliamentary democracy in England: "The people of England regards itself as free: but it is grossly mistaken: it is free only during the election of members of parliament. As soon as they are elected, slavery overtakes it, and it is nothing. The use it makes of the short moments of liberty it enjoys shows indeed that it deserves to lose them." Rousseau, *Social Contract,* 94.

26. John Dewey, *The Public and Its Problems* (Chicago: The Swallow Press, 1954), 147.

27. Rousseau, *Discourse on the Origins,* 265.

28. Jefferson, "Letter to Peter Carr," in *Portable Jefferson,* 424–25.

29. Benjamin Barber goes so far as to argue that politics itself must take up the questions of epistemology in the absence of certainty. Politics becomes the very grounding for epistemological certainty missing from any metaphysical schema; Barber, *Strong Democracy,* chap. 8.

30. Rousseau, *Social Contract,* 65.

31. Small face-to-face associations may, however, also facilitate the suppression of some issues, or the pressing for a false consensus by those with greater power, and in smaller groups, more latent powers such as rhetorical persuasiveness may tip the balance in favor of some over others in the community; see Mansbridge, *Beyond Adversary Democracy,* 34.

32. Warren, *Democracy and Poetry,* 14.

33. Given the complexities and interdependence that characterize modern mass polities, small groups may not be adequate to handling large scale problems. It may be that only centralized political institutions can cope with contemporary political

problems, which would wreak havoc on the participatory-republican ideal of small face-to-face political association; see Mansbridge, *Beyond Adversary Democracy,* 279–81, for a discussion of this dilemma.

34. Rousseau, *Social Contract,* 65.

35. Finley, *Democracy: Ancient and Modern,* 102–3.

36. Rousseau, *Social Contract,* 88. In other passages, however, Rousseau is pessimistic about the possibilities of constituting democracy. In a passage similar to Federalist no. 51, he argues: "Were there a people of gods, their government would be democratic. So perfect a government is not for men" (Ibid., III, iv, 66).

37. Jefferson, "Letter to John Adams," in *Portable Jefferson,* 538.

38. Ibid., 533–39.

39. Benjamin Barber, "Command Performance," *Harpers* (April 1975): 52.

40. James MacGregor Burns, *Leadership* (New York: Harper and Row, Publishers, 1979), 439, 448. See also the discussion of the relationship between the republican leader and the teacher in the classroom below, Part II, Chapter 8.

41. Aristotle, *Politics,* 93.

42. Thomas Jefferson, "Letter to Joseph Cabell," in *The Writings of Thomas Jefferson,* ed. H. A. Washington (Washington: Taylor and Maury, 1854), 6: 543–44.

43. Jefferson, "Letter to Edward Everett" (March 27, 1824), in *Writings,* 8: 341.

44. Dewey, *Democracy and Education,* 9.

45. Ibid., 87.

46. Jean-Jacques Rousseau, *The Government of Poland* (Indianapolis: Bobbs-Merrill Educational Publishing, 1972), 30.

47. Horace Mann, "The Necessity of Education in a Republican Government," in *Lectures on Education* (New York: Arno Press, 1969), 124–25.

48. Dewey, *Democracy and Education,* 87.

49. Ibid.

50. Rousseau, *Emile,* 38.

51. Ibid., 325.

52. Ibid., 327.

53. Robert McClintock, *Man and His Circumstances: Ortega as Educator* (New York: Teacher's College Press, 1971), 53–54.

54. See Allan Bloom's introduction to Rousseau's *Emile,* 11.

55. Rousseau, *Emile,* 41. Given the corrupt society responsible for making such "double men," *Emile* is meant to show a private, "domestic education" able to make a living, acting man within corrupt, modern society. Hegel, however, argues against the strategy laid out in *Emile:* "The educational experiments, advocated by Rousseau, in *Emile,* of withdrawing children from the common life of everyday and bringing them up in the country, have turned out to be futile, since no success can attend an attempt to estrange people from the laws of the world . . . It is by becoming a citizen of a good state that the individual first comes into his right"; Hegel, *Philosophy of Right,* 261.

56. Rousseau, "Political Economy," in Cole, *Social Contract and Discourses,* 308.

57. Aristotle, *Ethics,* 309–11.

58. Rousseau, *Political Economy,* 309.

59. Dewey, "My Pedagogic Creed," 21–22.

60. Rousseau, *Emile,* 48, 80–90.

61. Ibid., 251, 161.

62. Dewey, "My Pedagogic Creed," 30.

63. See Dewey, *Democracy and Education,* 186.

64. This is Aristotle's argument in *Politics,* 5–6, 233.

65. Rousseau, *Discourse on the Origins,* 281–82.

66. Rousseau, "Discourse on the Arts and Sciences," in Cole, *Social Contract and Discourses,* 173.

67. Dewey, *Public and Its Problems,* p. 207.

68. Hannah Pitkin argues that the kind of moral autonomy that the individual develops through political life and activity is similar to Kant's notion of personal "lawmaking," in that the individual sets norms and principles by which he or she acts based on interpersonal and universal reasoning and extrapolation. The difference is that this ethical norm-setting is not conducted internally, as for Kant, but externally, "with the actual experience of making, administering, and altering of the norms by which the community lives—not just by oneself, privately, in the mind, but with one's fellow citizens, in deliberation, debate, political maneuvering and conflict". See Hannah Pitkin, "Justice: On Relating Public and Private," *Political Theory* (May 1981).

69. Dewey, *Democracy and Education,* 275–76.

70. For discussions of the strength of "participatory-republican" ideas in American political thought, see J. G. A. Pocock, *The Machiavellian Moment* (Princeton: Princeton University Press, 1975), chap. 15, and the discussion of America's two "constitutional traditions" in W. C. McWilliams, "The American Constitutions," in *The Performance of American Government* (New York: Free Press, 1972), 1–45.

71. "Letter to Joseph Cabell," in *Writings of Thomas Jefferson,* 543–44.

72. Thomas Jefferson, "Letter to Samuel Kerchival (July 12, 1816)," in Jefferson, *Writings* 7: 9–17; "Letter to John Cartwright, (June 5, 1824)," in Ibid., 358.

73. Thomas Jefferson, "Letter to Wiliam Jarvis (September 28, 1820)," in Ibid., 179.

74. Quoted in *Crusade Against Ignorance: Thomas Jefferson on Education,* ed. Gordon C. Lee (Teachers College Press, Columbia University, 1961), 19. Jefferson wanted to proclaim "a crusade against ignorance; to establish and improve the law for educating the common people." See "Letter to George Washington (January 4, 1786)," in *Memoirs, Correspondence and Miscellanies From the Papers of Thomas Jefferson,* vol. 1, ed. T. J. Randolph (Boston: Gray and Bowen, 1830), 394.

75. Thomas Jefferson, "Letter to Kerchival," in *Writings,* 14.

PART II

The Education of Democratic Citizens

Curricular Policies and Practices in American High Schools

CHAPTER 3

Goals of Civic Education
Limited Knowledge and Participation

N OW THAT WE HAVE COMPLETED our discussion of the two major conceptions of democratic politics and citizenship and their general implications for political education, it remains our task to explore contemporary issues in public schooling in America which affect the education of citizens. The question of how one goes about educating democratic citizens will be examined by looking at the current curricular wisdom and practices in America's secondary schools in light of the prior discussion of what it means to be a democratic citizen. We will examine first how the aims of citizen education have been defined among American educational thinkers and practitioners. Then we will look at the entire curriculum, including what is called the "hidden curriculum" of the schools. We will also explore problems relating to the connection between subject matter and method, the use of texts, cognitive and affective content in the curriculum, and proposals for structural educational reform as they affect civic education. We will close Part II with a discussion of the teacher's proper role in citizenship education.

As we proceed, we must remember the caveat made in the introduction about addressing questions of educational practice in a vacuum. Where possible, we will try to link our examination of the schools and citizen education to a wider social context. Still, it is worth reiterating that the prominence of the schools in teaching future citizens dictates a careful look at their policies and practices in their own context. Though constantly aware of the limits of an analysis of schools alone, we must be urged on by the importance of tackling an issue that, in its entirety, has been left unaddressed for so long.

American educators have not been wont to discuss the general aims of education in any specific or thorough fashion, and this tends to be especially true of the aims of citizen education. Many of our contemporary educational writers would agree with James Conant, a major influence on educational practices in the high schools, who said that "a sense of distasteful weariness overtakes" him at the mention of any discussion of educational philosophy or goals. "In such a mood," he continues, "I am ready to define education as what goes on in schools and colleges."[1] But as boring and unappealing as such a discussion might be, it is important to understand how educators conceive of the major aims and purposes in citizenship training (when they do take up general goals as a subject of discourse) before moving on to particular curricular practices. If there are major problems in the way we define the overall task of citizen education, given what it means to be a democratic citizen, these deficiencies will certainly inform many of the concrete policies and proposals in the curriculum. We may want to separate problems with the way citizenship goals are conceived from problems in the actual carrying out of these goals in curricular practice.

Although norms and behavior appropriate to good citizenship have always been a concern of American educators, their importance became paramount at the beginning of the twentieth century. The large influx of immigrants in the late nineteenth and early twentieth century, especially those from southern and eastern Europe, was beginning to be seen as creating a "national problem" (the U.S. Immigration Commission's study in 1909 showed that 58 percent of children in schools of the nation's largest cities were of foreign-born parentage), and the effort to "Americanize" these immigrants was a major task of the public schools in the early 1900s.[2] Partly informed by felt inadequacies of the secondary schools in meeting the needs and challenges created by this large influx of students from foreign cultures, the National Education Association's

Commission on the Reorganization of Secondary Education published a report entitled *Cardinal Principles of Secondary Education*
in 1918. This report set down a number of general goals for the
secondary schools which remained strong influences for decades,
informing educational thinking well into the 1960s. The Commission decided that secondary school education should fulfill two basic
functions: that of specialization, "whereby individuals may become
effective in the various vocations and other fields of human endeavor"; and unification, or "the attainment of those common ideas,
common ideals, and common modes of thought, feeling, and action
that make for cooperation, social cohesion, and social solidarity."[3] In
order to fulfill these basic functions, the Commission's report sin-
gled out seven specific goals which secondary schools should pursue: health, command of fundamental processes, worthy home-
membership, vocation, citizenship, worthy use of leisure time, and
ethical character.

While *Cardinal Principles of Secondary Education* does affirm
citizenship to be a major goal of secondary education, and while it
considers "social solidarity" to be a desirable outcome of education,
the Commission's report defines citizenship in very vague terms, as
"law-abiding behavior" and as acceptance of given standards and
norms. The components of criticism and discussion and of active
participation are left out of the Commission's definition of democratic citizenship. Thus, though seeming to promote affective ties to
the polity as a crucial factor in citizenship, this report fails to recognize the foundations of affective ties in political participation, which
characterize the participatory-republican conception of the democratic citizen.

But *Cardinal Principles* also neglects the cognitive components of
citizenship found in both the liberal and participatory-republican
conceptions. The report makes no reference to the universal development of intellectual capacity or the cognitive mastery of
academic subjects which characterized earlier proposals about the
aims of education (most notably the Report From the Committee of
Ten, headed by Charles Elliot in 1893). The main task of the high
school was "to help in the wise choice of a vocation." This was best
served by a course of studies which was "individually useful," not a
"bookish curricula" which would lead "tens of thousands of boys and

girls away from the pursuits for which they are adapted."[4] While earlier discussions of goals conceived of a "universal academic education," *Cardinal Principles* ushered in a period in which vocational training was to become the metaphor for democratic education in America. Conceived in this way, this major influence on the laying out of proper goals of secondary education neglects the cognitive foundations of common belief and values, as well as the competency skills necessary to democratic citizenship.[5]

The next major re-examination of national goals for secondary schooling did not come until 1973, when the National Commission on the Reform of Secondary Education published its report, *The Reform of Secondary Education*. (Two studies which led to recommendations for secondary education and its aims were done in the intervening years, but the first did not contain material significantly different from the *Cardinal Principles,* and the second refrained from making grand claims about the goals of education.)[6] The goals expressed in *The Reform of Secondary Education* move further away from a *primary* concern with citizenship or the collective values necessary to it. There is a much heavier emphasis than in times past on narrowly utilitarian goals of education, toward developing the cognitive skills and knowledge necessary for moving oneself ahead in the economic and social system. The concern with vocational specialization, with "occupational competence," that runs through this later report is far greater than in the *Cardinal Principles,* which as mentioned above, helped start the trend toward vocational studies.

While the *Cardinal Principles* may have had a limited notion of citizenship, it still maintained the necessity of common values and the centrality of citizenship education (even if much of it was a euphemism for the Americanization of foreign-born students); and in its promotion of vocational education it still held that the diverse curricula offered in the school should be housed in the single "comprehensive high school," so that students could be exposed to persons with different backgrounds and intellectual interests under the same roof. *The Reform of Secondary Education* concerns itself mostly with knowledge to serve individual purposes, with the development of "ethical character" in individuals being replaced by the "clarification of one's values" (values clarification and its implications for citizenship are discussed in chapter 4), and with "social solidarity" being replaced by "appreciation of others," which calls for tolerance and the ability to get along with one's fellow citizens, but does not require positive solidarity.[7]

Moreover, *The Reform of Secondary Education* recommends greater individualized instruction in secondary schools, promotes the specialization of schooling opportunities for those with different interests, and moves away from the housing of those with different interests in the same educational community. The ramifications of specialized instruction on citizenship are great; instead of the comprehensive high school which houses students from all backgrounds and interests, the policy recommendations outlined in this report would severely segregate and isolate students according to educational and vocational interest. James Conant understood the *political* need for maintaining the comprehensive high school: "It is important for the future of American democracy to have as close a relationship as possible in high school between the future professional man, the future craftsman, the future manager of industry, the future labor leader, the future salesman, and the future engineer."[8]

This report demonstrates a concern for citizenship as a national goal, but its view of citizenship is even more narrowly circumscribed than that of the 1918 report. Again, the report does little to promote active participation as a requirement of democratic citizenship, even to protect one's interests in today's complex society (which would be a possible goal of citizen education even under the liberal conception). Under a conception which follows from these goals as they are articulated, citizens would be expected to respect law and authority, as well as property and the opinions of others, without any elaboration of the affective bonds or collective values which should underly respect for fellow citizens, law, or political authority. Moreover, the citizenship goals as specified in the report do not include the teaching of any particular areas of cognitive knowledge (and very few skills) appropriate to citizenship.

But it must be understood that *The Reform of Secondary Education* is typical of recent trends in thinking about general goals of citizen education in the high schools. On one hand, there is a prominent school of thought which holds that *any* political or citizenship aims are illegitimate to the enterprise of education, since they are imposed from without upon the process of education or upon certain curricula which then lose their distinctive *intrinsic* character.[9] Recently, Patricia Graham argued that education has been too often justified by its "social purposes," such as instilling a sense of civic responsibility, of patriotism, or of morality. Graham sees little need to discuss goals of political value in secondary education; she proposes that we conceive of the sole aim of education as promoting the limited cognitive goal of literacy, defined as the capacity to read, communicate, compute, and make judgments. This is the only legitimate curricular goal in the current educational crisis in America, according to Graham.[10]

On the other hand, there is a school of thought (which represents the majority of current educational writers) which says that citizenship goals are important, if not primary, to the nature of secondary schooling, but which has a limited notion of citizen education. A number of reports reflecting this school of thought, from centers for citizenship and task forces studying citizenship, have been released in the past ten years. All have defined citizenship values in terms of cognitive knowledge and attitudes necessary for a limited participation in politics. All stress the need for future citizens to acquire knowledge about the "principal issues in contemporary society," about one's stake in these issues, about the skills and competencies needed if one wants to work with or in governmental institutions, "in order to protect and promote one's interests and values." In addition, most of these educational thinkers include as important the ability to make judgments on and appraisals of evidence presented in political disputes, and the appreciation of the rights, opinions, and interests of others "in a diverse and pluralistic society."[11]

But their notions of citizenship go no farther than this. The failure of the President's Commission on Excellence in Education (1983) specifically to address citizenship education goals has already been described in the introduction. The only goals the Commission has set have to do with concrete content and proficiency standards for students and teachers. The only admonition to the schools in the area of civic education is to help students "fix their places" in society, "understand . . . ideas that have shaped our world" and "how our political system functions," and "grasp the difference between free and repressive societies."[12] These are very narrow and functional citizen education goals, and are narrowly seen as being the province solely of social studies teachers.

Even those studies which have proposed solid and coherent curricula in line with the promotion of civic competence have fallen short in their articulation of the goals of civic instruction. Fred Newmann and associates, who offer a comprehensive curriculum which integrates various courses of study into a coherent citizen education program in a way that few other programs or proposals do (see chapter 4), still conceive of the goals of citizenship very narrowly. They understand citizenship as "the ability to exert influence in public affairs," under a liberal, interest-oriented conception of politics. But even within this narrow conception of citizenship, Newmann and his colleagues believe that the objective of citizen education should be only to "increase the *ability* to exert [political] influence." They feel that it is completely proper that "some may *choose to use it only sparingly* (emphasis added)."[13] This argument is very similar to that of the modern liberal-democrats discussed above, who greatly circumscribe mass citizen participation in the belief that citizens may be most "rational" when uninvolved in the political arena.

Even the most promising of the recent high school studies, in terms of its suggestions for curricular practice (from the standpoint of citizen education), lacks depth in its conception of goals. The Carnegie Foundation's report on American secondary education,[14] headed by Ernest Boyer, is a positive step toward articulating the proper purposes of public education. Boyer and his colleagues propose "four essential goals" for secondary education which go a long way toward simply defining the future tasks of American high schools. These include the development of critical thinking and communication capacities, a learning about oneself and the "human heritage" through a "core curriculum," and the drive to "help all students fulfill their social and civic obligations through school and community service."[15] But from the standpoint of civic education, the goals articulated by this report do not flesh out a coherent conception of what it means to be a citizen. Nor is any further elaboration of citizenship goals included in the more concrete discussion of the curriculum, apart from the need to eradicate "civic illiteracy."[16] So the Carnegie Foundation report, too, misses the mark when it comes to the coherent discussion of the goals of civic education.

In the most recent discussions of curricular goals in secondary schooling, then, where citizenship goals are discussed at all, they are basically reflective of liberal notions of citizenship. Citizens are seen as people who know the laws of the state and uphold them, and who get involved in the political realm only to the extent necessary to promote and protect their interests. The goals of secondary education are outlined as being to provide such citizens with the cognitive skills and knowledge necessary to carry out these limited functions, and to instill in them the cognitive values of tolerance and respect for others consistent with liberal recognition of the subjectivity of interests and the equality of people's claims upon the political realm.

On the whole, these curricular goals fail to incorporate important elements of the participatory-republican conception of democratic citizenship. The thinkers described above do not include among the goals of citizen education developing persons who are at once autonomous and yet recognize their dependence on others around them, nor do they include helping people affirm affective bonds and common values shared with others in the immediate political community. Even the attributes of active participation and vibrant interpersonal discussion, as these might be understood by participatory-republicans, are not proclaimed as citizen virtues to be instilled by the schools. Thus a major current of American thought about democratic citizenship, participation, and political community is not reflected in any significant way in even the general goals of secondary education as laid out by contemporary educators. The revitalization of this conception of democratic politics and citizenship seems crucial to our better functioning as a democratic polity, and therefore requires a rethinking of the goals we set for citizenship education in our secondary schools.

But since statements about general goals do not describe the whole curriculum, and sometimes do not even encompass the actual curricular practices in the schools, it is necessary to look at specific curricular theory and policy as they affect citizen education in American high schools. We need to see what further implications can be drawn from examining the civics curriculum in some detail, given our understanding of what it means to be a democratic citizen under each alternative conception. For purposes of analysis, we have divided the various topics of the "civics curriculum" into separate sections. It should be recognized, however, that the various issues are integrally related to one another, and that the "curriculum" of the democratic citizen should properly be understood in its entirety. At the conclusion of this study, we will attempt to synthesize the various segments of the curriculum discussed in the following chapters into a picture of the whole of civic education in the secondary schools.

NOTES

1. Quoted in Silberman, *Crisis in the Classroom,* 6.

2. Lawrence Cremin, *The Transformation of the School: Progressivism in American Education* (New York: Alfred A. Knopf, 1961), 66–75.

3. Commission on the Reorganization of Secondary Education, *Cardinal Principles of Secondary Education* (Bulletin 1918, no. 35, Washington: U.S. Government Printing Offices, 1918), 16.

4. Ibid.

5. See Frances Fitzgerald's criticism in *America Revised: History Schoolbooks in the Twentieth Century* (Boston: Little, Brown, and Co., 1979), 168–71.

6. The first study was done in 1938 by the Education Policies Commission of the NEA and the American Association of School Administrators, entitled *The Purposes of Education in American Democracy* (Washington: NEA and AASA, 1938). The second was James Conant's landmark study, *The American High School Today* (New York: McGraw-Hill, 1959).

7. National Commission on the Reform of Secondary Education, *The Reform of Secondary Education* (New York: McGraw-Hill, 1973), 31–34. *The Reform of Secondary Education* also recommended dropping requirements on compulsory attendance after age fourteen, which would make it more difficult to bring adolescents of all backgrounds together to learn the lessons of democratic citizenship. The *Cardinal Principles* recommended that students in secondary schools normally remain at least part-time until age eighteen.

8. James Conant, *The Comprehensive High School* (New York: McGraw-Hill, 1967), 62.

9. See, for example, R. S. Peters, "Aims of Education: A Conceptual Inquiry," in Peters, ed., *The Philosophy of Education* (Oxford University Press, 1973), 11–57, especially 16–21. See also Irving Morrissett, "Romance and Realism in Citizenship Education," *The Social Studies* 72, no. 1 (1981): 15–17.

10. Patricia Alberg Graham, "Literacy: A Goal for Secondary Schools," *Daedalus* (Summer 1981): 119–134.

11. Examples of this school of thought include the U.S. Office of Education's National Panel on High School and Adolescent Education, whose report *The Education of Adolescents* (Washington: U.S. Government Printing Office, 1976) includes a segment on citizenship (see 10ff); The National Task Force on Citizenship Education's *Education for Responsible Citizenship* (see Brown's introductory essay); and Richard Remy's "Criteria for Judging Citizenship's Education Programs," *Education Leadership* (October 1980): 10–11.

12. President's Commission, *A Nation At Risk*, 25–26.

13. Fred Newmann, et al., *Skills in Citizen Action: An English-Social Studies Program for Secondary Schools* (Madison: University of Wisconsin Publications, 1977), 5–6.

14. Ernest Boyer *High School.*

15. Ibid., 66–67.

16. Ibid., 105.

CHAPTER 4

The Explicit Curriculum
of the Democratic Citizen

C ITIZENSHIP EDUCATION in American high schools is conducted almost exclusively through the social studies curriculum. Social studies classes have long been the place in
American high schools where students are taught the traits and
skills that make up "good citizenship." But this is not to say that the
character of civics instruction has remained unchanged—indeed,
since the beginning of the century, curricular theory and practice in
the social studies have undergone a number of major changes.

At the turn of the century, history was the disciplinary vehicle by
which students were brought to an understanding of the values and
behavior underlying democratic citizenship. Educators of the time
argued that history was "the repository of the great classical ideas
and ideals of humankind that were prerequisite to effective democratic citizenship," and was thus the only course of study needed to
sufficiently "discipline the faculties of the mind" in preparation for
entrance into the world of democratic politics.[1] The Committee of
Seven of the American Historical Association (1899) recommended a
four-stage sequence in history that would constitute the entirety of
the social studies and the civics curriculum in high school: ancient
history in ninth grade, medieval and modern history in tenth, English history in eleventh grade, and American history and civil government in twelfth grade. The object was for the student to master a
body of historical facts—names, dates, and events in political, diplo-

matic, and military history—to be "learned by heart, and when forgotten, learned again."[2] These recommendations were strongly influential in the social studies curriculum almost universally into the 1920s, and in some cases into the 1940s.

By the 1920s, however, social studies educators began to dismiss "history for the sake of history" as the dominant mode of instruction in the civics curriculum. They argued that in order to help students become good citizens now and in the future, a curriculum more relevant to current political situations and social relationships needed to be developed. What came out of the criticism from these (mostly "progressive") social studies educators was the practice of dividing the high school curricula into a history sequence, consisting of memorizable content as before, but streamlined into one course in world history and one in American history, and a "problems of democracy" course (or something like it) in the twelfth grade, where students would analyze and familiarize themselves with contemporary political and social issues. History was somewhat separated from that part of the social studies curriculum which specifically dealt with citizenship education.[3] The "problems of democracy" approach to civics instruction is still used in many schools today.

But findings from public surveys in the 1940s made people question whether this "social problems" approach was valid for teaching citizen values. It was found that high school graduates, whether or not they had taken social studies courses, were unable to recall important facts about American history and government. To the results of the various studies were added the launching of Sputnik and more survey findings in the 1950s showing that young Americans did not universally support the democratic values of free speech, assembly, due process, and toleration of divergent political viewpoints.[4] The high schools and their civics curricula were put under attack for a failure to provide proper citizenship training, which led to another transformation in the social studies curriculum in the 1960s, with the creation of "the new social studies."

Spurred on by federal funding, the new thrust in curricular practice was to teach courses in the separate disciplines comprising "social science." It was felt that to shore up the previously "soft" social studies (also called "social slush" and "social stew" by critics), students should be taught the scientific method of inquiry used in the study of each of the social science disciplines, in effect making them junior sociologists, political scientists, psychologists, and geographers. Representatives from each social science discipline (in universities) developed separate units to be plugged into the social studies curriculum in the high schools, usually consisting of mini-versions of texts and materials used at the university level.[5] These educators believed that not only was the study of the academic social science disciplines by high school students good in itself, but that it would also produce better, more informed citizens. Bernard Berelson justified the study of academic social science disciplines this way: "We want to give high school students the best introduction we can, within limits of practicality, to the best available knowledge from the social science disciplines *as a means* to the end of producing responsible citizens (emphasis added)."[6]

For these social scientists, then, citizenship would be improved "when people have learned how to look at the world through the eyes of social scientists."[7] The "social science disciplines" approach to the social studies curriculum, though it has lost much of its initial impact, still informs many school programs in civic education. In fact, many schools have discarded their twelfth grade government or "problems of democracy" courses in favor of social science electives, such as sociology and psychology.[8]

Critics have argued that the "new social studies" reforms of the 1960s made the civics curriculum much too subject-centered. Educators have attempted to get students to master the contents and approaches of social science disciplines, with no attention paid to substantive values (social science is, after all, value free!). Edwin Fenton, one of the founding fathers of the "new social studies," argued that only "procedural values" (that is, attitudes of rational thought), and not substantive values, should be taught in the schools. He and other educators considered it illegitimate to do anything more than teach students "how to analyze questions of substantive value."[9] However, any method of civic education which does not teach the substantive values that underlie democratic citizenship seems far out of keeping with either participatory-republican or liberal conceptions of political education. For participatory-republicans, the creation of common bonds necessary to a participatory democratic politics depends upon the learning of substantive values which undergird the political community. And even liberals see certain values, such as respect for law, toleration, and freedom, as the foundations of the political and social order, and believe that these must be taught consciously to the young.

A concern that values were being neglected in the social studies curriculum led to the development in the past decade of two alternate approaches in civic education—values clarification and moral development. The values clarification approach centers on encouraging students to examine standards and guides which underlie their everyday behavior, to understand the process of choosing among and committing themselves to certain values and then acting on them, and to respect the values and commitments made by others. Advocates of values clarification believe that people who have rationally examined and chosen their values after discussion and challenge in the classroom will be better citizens, since many civic problems result from confusion over values. But the values clarification approach focuses instruction only on "the process of valuing, not on the transmission of the 'right' set of values." It is a highly personal process, in which teachers merely try to get individual students to think about and "clarify" what they value—with no one student's values having greater merit than another's. Sidney Simon, a major proponent of values clarification, argues that it is illegitimate to attempt to inculcate, instill, or foster values, having come to "the realization that all the inculcating, instilling, and fostering added up to indoctrination."[10] There is very little discussion of politics or the development of collective or community values in any of the values clarification literature, even though this is purportedly a method of civic education—in fact, values clarification is predicated upon the belief that there are no common values (for certain), given all the diversity we find around us.[11]

The values clarification approach to citizenship education reflects the liberal concern (as discussed in Part I) over the possibility that the teaching of common political values will produce men and women who uniformly and uncritically accept a set of imposed beliefs, thus resulting in an endangerment to liberal freedom. Many contemporary advocates of values clarification techniques feel that the instilling of common norms of behavior will enforce the status quo, stifling social change and forcing minorities to acquire the values of white middle class society. But this scenario seems over-drawn, given that there is a critical, cognitive component to any conception of democratic citizenship education. If, as participatory-republicans contend, political community is possible only where people are bound together by a common reverence for the same conception of politics, justice, and virtue, the instilling of common values and purposes is necessary as a foundation for doing anything politically, whether it be reforming or preserving the status quo. In fact, the internalizing of principles of equality, democratic participation, freedom, and diversity which make up the core of democratic politics should lead to a keener awareness of problems and tensions within the practice of these principles, and to a motivation to act in changing such practices when needed. Moreover, it seems more damaging to "minority values" to argue condescendingly, as much of the values clarification literature and materials does, that some people are "legitimate" in valuing lawlessness, disrespect for authority, indolence, or selfishness, rather than to challenge them to search together for common sets of values.[12]

The moral development approach to citizenship education comes out of Lawrence Kohlberg's research into the stages of cognitive moral development. Kohlberg argues that people think in qualitatively different ways about moral issues, progressing from pre-conventional and conventional modes of thought to more principled stages of moral thinking in the course of cognitive development over time in their lives. Given that the highest stages of moral thinking reflect attitudes toward justice, rights, and liberty that are most appropriate to citizenship, the object of the curriculum ought to be to facilitate progress in a person's moral development. Kohlberg and his associates have found that initiating moral discussions about hypothetical or real moral dilemmas helps students confront moral issues and their thinking about them which then facilitates their movement to higher stages of cognitive moral development. These findings have led to proposals and programs which use "moral development methods" as the primary guide to instruction in the social studies.[13]

The moral development approach represents a refreshing attitude toward civic education. This approach begins to be concerned with the total curriculum as it affects moral and citizenship education, not just social studies classes. The moral development curriculum includes a strong participatory element, involving students directly in governing themselves through community meetings within the schools (although Kohlberg and his associates chalk up all the beneficial results of participation in school to the "better moral atmosphere developed in a school based firmly on the findings of research in cognitive moral development"[14] rather than the more probable conclusion that participation in a community of peers brings with it affective as well as cognitive bonds to others and a sense of self that positively change one's attitudes and behavior). Kohlberg's civics curriculum also stresses cognitive skills that are important to any notion of citizenship, and emphasizes doing away with parts of the "hidden curriculum" which teach radically different lessons from the overt curriculum (discussed in further detail in the next chapter).

But serious problems also exist in this approach to citizen education. First of all, most of the suggested moral dilemmas and discussions to be used in high school classroom settings are of an interpersonal nature (e.g., should Jill turn in her friend Sharon for cheating/stealing, or, should a Christian girl in Nazi Germany hide a Jewish friend from the Gestapo and thereby jeopardize her own family). The dilemmas presented are not very complex in nature and do not usually involve any larger social or political group; that is to say, there is little *political* content to most of the moral issue discussions proposed in this approach. In addition, the thrust of the moral development literature denies that part of citizenship characterized by caring for the affairs of one's community and by the mutual sharing of concern among community members which makes people able to engage in common political *action*. The overriding thrust of the advocates of moral development is with fostering cognitive skills and competencies, not with the important affective foundations, recognized by participatory-republicans, for working out public policy disputes. In fact, by attempting to attach people to abstract universal principles of justice and right, Kohlberg's method of instruction may even have the effect of *extricating* people from localized bonds of community and political commitment, as these are seen as being too "parochial."

Finally, again from a participatory-republican point of view, the "universal" ethical principles which make up Kohlberg's highest stage of moral development ("Stage Six") and which are the basis for his vision of good citizenship seem little distinct from the hardly universal liberal political principles. Stage Six is characterized by a sense of self-esteem, concern for one's rights and liberties (compatible with those of others, of course), adherence to principles of contract, free agreement, and consent, and the political belief in individual participation (one person, one vote) and the sanctity of individual conscience in conflictual political matters. By presenting ethical responses characteristic of the highest stage of moral development as universally valid, the moral development school merely attempts to give grounding and certainty to the disputed liberal principles of political right, which according to participatory-republicans, make up only a part of the picture of democratic politics and citizenship.

Other major curricular approaches to citizen education have been proposed and are in practice in the schools, but these four ("problems of democracy," "social science disciplines," "values clarification," and "moral development") constitute the bulk of current educational wisdom and practice. Yet despite all of these curricular innovations over the past twenty-five years, most observers agree that the burden of teaching citizenship in the high school curriculum still lies on narrowly conceived social studies courses, which for the most part have failed to generate student interest, involvement, or competence in political life.[15] A cross-national study contends that no matter what has happened in the way of curricular reform, the still relatively small amount of time devoted to civic education makes it impossible to cover all the major areas of study, and that as a result students are not able to demonstrate all of the cognitive and affective traits that make up the democratic citizen.[16]

An Integrated Social Studies Curriculum

The problem with much of the curricular reform of the past two decades is that it was university-based and grew out of a dissatisfaction with the teaching method or contents of particular subjects, so that new proposals and projects were added to existing curricula: reformers "never really attacked the curriculum as a whole."[17]

Moreover, the tendency in teacher-training programs is to prepare future social studies instructors in individual subject areas, such as history, geography, economics, or government, without integrating them all into one curriculum or bringing in other fields which might be relevant to citizenship.[18] Phillip Jackson argues that this lack of integration is reflected in the cafeteria or supermarket-style atmosphere which is found in the high schools generally, where it is assumed that "variety and innovation are desirable qualities in a high school curriculum," and a high school is thought to be improved because "it offers more courses" now than it did previously.[19] But while more than 250 courses are offered in some high schools, basic citizenship skills and values go unlearned.

The lack of an integrated approach is the major problem with most of the current practices in the schools, and in some ways this reflects a liberal conception of education. Just as liberal psychology and politics deal in the aggregation of separate phenomena (whether they be interests, persons, or desires) to form "the whole," so too does the dominant philosophy in the schools add up each separate course of study to arrive at "the whole" of the curriculum. Multiple interests and approaches in education set up separate specialized courses or programs which do not interpenetrate in school even though they do in reality. When the requirements necessary for "complete citizenship" are perceived as not being met by the school, a new course of study is added; educators demonstrate a lack of concern with the overall education or curriculum of a student as it affects citizenship training, or even with better integrating the aggregate subject material that presently exists. John Dewey was aware of this tendency in the curriculum over fifty years ago:

> The tendency to assign separate values to each study and to regard the curriculum in its entirety as a kind of composite made by the aggregation of segregated values is a result of the isolation of social groups and classes. Hence it is the business of the schools in a democratic social group to struggle against this isolation in order that the various interests (different courses of study) may reinforce and play into one another.[20]

Dewey believed the curriculum should be organized so that "the student is systematically led to utilize his earlier lessons to help understand the present one, and also to use the present to throw additional light upon what has already been acquired." A good curriculum, he said, is one that "puts the student in the habitual attitude of finding points of contact and mutual bearings" between his or her separate classes and between the "comprehensive material of direct instruction" and "the realities of everyday life."[21]

We must now explore the prospects for and implications of the high school curriculum in light of the educational needs of democratic citizenship. In this exploration we will be guided by the implicit demands of our two conceptions of democratic citizenship, and by a tradition of political thinkers who understood the need to think holistically about the political education of a country's citizens.

The first need is to consider the integration of the social studies curriculum, since it is acknowledged by all to be the primary medium of citizen education in the secondary schools. One of the unfortunate (though consciously intended, as we saw above) results of the various reforms in social studies was the detachment of *history* from the main body of civic instruction. Current curricular approaches—ranging from the attempt to add rigor to the disciplines of the social studies by studying the concepts and techniques of social scientists, to the focus on contemporary problems, "moral dilemmas," or the "process of valuing"—have emphasized the contemporary and the transhistorical to the neglect of the historical perspective of politics. A rigorous understanding of history appears essential to any understanding of current events and problems, social science concepts, or the development of values and moral judgment. But where the study of history has been present at all in the high schools, it is either subsumed in social science or made unappealing and irrelevant by being offered as a mere parade of facts, what some have called the "multiplication tables" of history.[22] History is more often separated completely from the "official" civics program, and considered to be prior in sequence but not directly related to courses in government or citizen education.

A thorough understanding of history is critical to the education of democratic citizens. Thinkers in the participatory-republican tradition held that history was one of the chief studies in preparation for citizenship (and life in general). Rousseau argued that the study of history would teach his character Emile of the workings of the human mind and heart and of human associations over time. History could properly distance Emile from the particular actions of "assembled men or peoples," and thus allow him to learn and to judge them in a disinterested way. Through history, Emile's teacher could

> show [him] men from afar, to show him them in other times or other places and in such a way that he can see the stage without ever being able to act on it. . . . It is by means of history that, without the lessons of philosophy, he will read the hearts of men; it is by means of history that he will see them, a simple spectator, disinterested and without passion, as their judge and not as their accomplice or accusor.[23]

History would not only teach Emile the collective genius and action of peoples in the past, but would enable him to compare peoples' ideals and speeches with their actions, a trait essential in preparing for citizenship:

> To know men, one must see them act. In society one hears them speak. They show their speeches and hide their actions. But in history their actions are unveiled, and one judges them on the basis of the facts. Even their talk helps in evaluating them, for in comparing what they do with what they say, one sees both what they are and what they want to appear to be. The more they disguise themselves, the better one knows them.[24]

Thomas Jefferson also felt that history lessons were critical parts of a public education which would make people able to judge their fellows' proclamations and actions, and thereby make them better "guardians of their own liberty":

> History, by appraising [people] of the past, will enable them to judge of the future; it will avail them of the experience of other times and other nations; it will qualify them as judges of the actions and designs of men; it will enable them to know ambition under every disguise it may assume; and knowing it, to defeat its views.[25]

If we follow Rousseau and Jefferson, a course of study which merely looks at contemporary governmental institutions and the principles behind them or at contemporary political problems, or one that attempts merely to develop a process of moral reasoning or valuing in individual students, neglects the important relationship between political principles and action as well as the historical context in which principles and institutions develop. A thorough historical understanding allows us to become better judges of current problems, institutions, and values by showing us similar political situations over time, where we can disinterestedly examine them in all of their complexity and with all of their ramifications. History as a method of attaining disinterestedness also appears useful to future citizens who will be asked to reach common agreement on policy in the midst of their own interests and prejudices.

Moreover, under the participatory-republican conception, a sense of history would be needed to provide the affective bonds and common political identities which undergird a democratic, conflict-transformation-oriented politics. The collective memories of past events, actions, heroes, villains, errors, triumphs, and important character traits and values must be strongly maintained, as well as constantly examined and interpreted in light of current political happenings. All of this is best provided by a civic education which incorporates the lessons of history. Because "there is an identity to the polity that gives coherence and content to being a citizen," and since the "tradition of a polity" needs to be ever present to "guide and direct an individual as he acts in the present,"[26] schools need to provide a rigorous critical history as a primary part of the education of the participatory-republican citizen.

But a historical understanding is also essential under a liberal conception of citizen education. Liberal-democratic citizenship is also well served by the proper sense of judgment and disinterestedness which is produced by historical study. And although liberals are not interested in creating the kinds of affective bonds and communal foundations to which the study of history might lend itself, they are still concerned that the values and habits of society be passed on to the young. Only history can provide students with a knowledge of social standards that have withstood the test of time and can inform current practice. For Locke, history was "the great mistress of prudence and civil knowledge," making the student who learned its lessons "informed in the principles and precepts of virtue, for the conduct of his life."[27]

It is clear, then, that history ought to be fully integrated into the civics curriculum and interwoven into the study of democratic political institutions and principles, rather than considered separately as

a dry memorization of facts. In addition, the social studies curriculum ought to integrate materials leading to the development of
communications and rhetorical skills. The importance of discussion
and debate to democratic politics, especially under a participatory-
republican conception, makes these verbal reasoning skills mandatory for future citizens. Stephen Bailey has argued that training in
"negotiating skills" should be a part of civics instruction. The rhetorical skills of persuasion and bargaining, the ability to come down
from a "concrete" fixed position to discover areas of common agreement, and the psychic capacity to compromise (which goes against
much of the American emphasis on winning, on holding fast to one's
beliefs and positions, on not compromising) are necessary citizen
attributes in a diverse society where conflict is seen as legitimate
but yet surmountable.[28] Moreover, dialogue and rhetorical reasoning skills may also be important tools in coming to an *understanding* of political phenomena and ideas. Both Plato and Aristotle
felt that the knowledge necessary to a full political life was acquired
only through the process of intellectual discussion, or dialectic.

We have seen that the social studies component of a civics curriculum in keeping with our two conceptions of democratic politics
ought to incorporate political and social history and communications
skills into the traditional government curriculum. Although no such
coherent integration of these crucial elements exists in current practice, one program which comes close has been articulated and in-
stalled on a limited basis. Fred Newmann and associates have offered a fairly coherent one-year civics program which incorporates
different aspects of the social studies as well as the English curriculum. The study of the "political-legal process," which currently
makes up the bulk of many government courses elsewhere, is combined with a "communications course" (intended to strengthen discussion and debate skills essential to the democratic decision-
making process), a "community service internship," and a "citizen
action project" (to provide for experience in individual and group
political action), as well as a literature course examining "persisting
issues in citizenship." But while this course of study does go a long
way in terms of offering an integrated social studies program, it still
suffers from the lack of a history component, something characteristic of most recent civics programs. There is no concrete incorpora-

tion of history into the civics program Newmann and associates offer.[29]

The "Good Book" for the "Good Citizen"

We have just examined current practices in the high school social studies program, their deficiencies in terms of developing democratic citizens, and what a "proper" social studies curriculum might include. But no discussion of the secondary school social studies curriculum would be complete without an examination of the use of texts and other instructional materials in the classroom. There may be serious problems, given the citizenship goals we want to foster (following from the two models of citizenship) and the preceding section on the proper social studies curriculum, in both the content of instructional materials and in the attitude taken toward them by educators. Before moving on to the broader curriculum, then, we must come to grips with the proper role and function of social studies texts.

The central instrument of instruction in the vast majority of today's high school civics classes is the standard history and/or government textbook. An Educational Testing Service study of college-bound students in the mid-1960s revealed that 85 percent did more than half of their social studies reading from a single text.[30] With all of the changes that have occurred in civics classes since then, a study commissioned by the National Science Foundation in 1976 concurred that the dominant instructional tool in social studies still continues to be the "conventional textbook."[31] Tightened school budgets (which rule out extra expenses for multi-media resources, computer-based materials, or even additional texts) and the influence of the "back-to-basics" movement guarantee that the civics textbook will probably retain its paramount teaching role.

What can be said in general about the content of these textbooks? Until recently, one text, *Magruder's American Government*, dominated the market in high school American government texts, and it still enjoys widespread use.[32] It proclaims as its "main purpose the description, analysis, and explanation of the American political system,"[33] and it is basically an encyclopedia of American institutions and historical facts. The text contains very little narrative history or interpretation of American political history, and almost no sense of real controversy or contention in the processes of American democracy.

This bring us to the first major problem with almost all the major high school social studies textbooks: the fact that they ignore the presence of conflict in American political and social history. One political socialization scholar has observed that "the conflict aspect of democracy tends to be de-emphasized in instructional materials at the elementary and secondary school levels in spite of the fact that its recognition is vital for a genuine understanding of democracy."[34] A look at government texts confirms this. In *Magruder's American Government*, a discussion of the "basic concepts of democracy" includes a section on the "necessity of compromise" but nothing on the centrality of conflict to democratic politics.[35] Another text recommended for use in the high schools, *Civics for Americans*, also fails to convey a sense of politics as an arena of conflict, of the clash of differing interests and opinions, and of public battle over policies and principles. In talking about the Vietnam War, this text's only reference to any domestic conflict over government policy was to mention matter-of-factly that "some people questioned if it really was in our interest to be fighting this war."[36]

To make sure these were not isolated examples, I did a survey of the content of the five government texts approved for the State of Texas in the 1980s.[37] Again, though some texts are better than others, they all tend to minimize the conflict dimension of democratic political life in America. Rosencranz and Chapin's *American Government* reflects the "new social studies" approach, and spends most of its time trying to develop "social science skills" rather than bringing out the conflict over interests and values in American politics.[38] Scholastic's *American Citizenship*, though much better in its approach than some of the more traditional texts, tends to confine conflict to the courts, where judges definitively resolve conflicting interests. Where political conflict is discussed, it is done blandly and factually, and there seems to be an avoidance of the discussion of *value* conflicts in American politics.

Perhaps the best example of this absence of conflict and contention in high school civics texts is found in Richard Gross's *American*

Citizenship: The Way We Govern. Though admirable in its approach and its stress on active citizen participation, the text fails to present political conflict adequately. In a section on civil rights, the text states that though the Constitution gives all persons the same rights as others,

> black people have not been allowed to use those rights. For many years, many black people were not permitted to vote. Black people were not given an equal chance in education, jobs, and housing. Since the 1950s, the federal government has worked to make sure that black people—and all Americans—get their rights. Congress, the executive branch, and the courts have worked especially hard to protect the rights of minority group members. All Americans have equal rights. The government is trying to make sure that all Americans are allowed to use their rights.[39]

From this paragraph, the reader gets no sense of the actual historical or political dynamics of conflict over equal rights in American history, how it was and is being resolved, nor the value questions represented by such conflict. As a result, an essential part of democratic politics and citizenship is lost.

In general, then, civics texts tend to gloss over conflict as an essential element of democratic politics in favor of the unanimity and consensus that they feel characterize the American polity. In this they neglect a crucial component in any conception of democratic citizenship: the notion that the political arena is an area of conflict, where differing interests and opinions clash and do public battle in the process of resolving (or transforming) their conflicts. Frances Fitzgerald has even concluded that American textbook history, "in its flatness and its uncritical conformism, is a kind of American Socialist Realism."[40]

Here we encounter a difficult paradox. While the textbook presentation of consensus in American politics would seem to promote some of the affective values which participatory-republicans aim at in their conception of political education, the complete absence of narratives about conflict misses the importance of the process by which the polity achieves consensus. As we saw above, the participatory-republican conception of democratic politics sees conflict between citizens as essential to the process of arriving at common community rules and norms. The flat presentation of American political unanimity in civics textbooks is not informed by a view of politics as *conflict transformation.*

In the section above we saw the importance of history as a central component of the future citizen's social studies curriculum. High school civics texts, however, are sorely deficient in their treatment of history. The institutional thrust of most government texts precludes providing a rich and complex historical context to political actions and institutions. Here the Rosencranz and Chapin text in *American Government* is a good case in point. In comparing and contrasting political and economic systems, the authors make little attempt to connect these conceptual categories to historical examples of such systems. And their attempt to introduce various theories of political scientists about the political process also fails to connect these theories to concrete historical practices.[41]

When history *is* introduced, it is covered as a series of simple facts; these texts offer little in the way of critical or intellectual history. This latter omission may be most crucial. Todd and Curti's *Rise of the American Nation,* a popular history textbook, is devoid of American *intellectual* history.[42] And though almost all of the high school government texts contain a few pages on different ideas about the nature of politics, most tend to be ahistorical in their discussion of these ideas.

Without a rich discussion of the history of debates and discussions carried out in America over ideas about society and politics, students receive no feeling for the foundations or the grounding of the American republic. A political community is built upon the goals, purposes, and visions that come out of the historical discussion of political ideas as well as particular policies and institutions. Textbooks failing to give American intellectual history the treatment it deserves "drain the soul out of American history."[43]

Some of the changes made in civics textbooks may have exacerbated rather than alleviated this problem with historical content. The use of "inquiry" or "discovery" texts, which has increased somewhat over the past decade, has encouraged in students a more active and critical stance toward the material and toward political issues discussed. But these inquiry texts also tend to ask questions out of their historical context, or to present so little of it as to make "active inquiry" meaningless. These texts also tend to assume no common values or standards to apply to the political issues or events discussed, believing (in good liberal fashion) in allowing the individual to establish his or her own.

Examples of this are rampant. In recent editions, *Magruder's American Government* has incorporated a "discovery" component, including some thirty-five case studies designed to provoke student inquiry and evaluation; but these case studies are little more than separated stories, and most of the suggested questions and activities designed in conjunction with the textual material are politically lifeless or historically irrelevant. Some examples of case studies in *Magruder* include boxed stories on "Sam Rayburn's Advice to New Members of Congress," data from poll results on citizens' "political information" and on "independent voters," and a story selecting quotes from various American presidents on their views of the presidency.[44] Some of the activities in which students are encouraged to engage include debates on "whether the framers of the Constitution should have provided for a unicameral Congress" or whether "presidents ought to become lifetime members of the Senate," and writing "an essay on the necessity of preventing World War III."[45]

Gross's *American Government,* Scholastic's *American Citizenship,* and Gillespie and Lazarus's *American Government: Comparing Political Experiences* also contain examples of the problems involved in attempting to make historical material relevant to contemporary students and susceptible to a critical and participatory reading on their part. The Gross text contains a section at the end of each chapter called "Issues in Government," meant to develop "skills . . . in practical problem solving." But most of these issues tend to be sanitized of any historical meaning. In one chapter, for instance, a question raised about whether the United States should "support revolutions in other countries" is presented as being completely unrelated to any historical context or situation.[46] Similarly, Scholastic's *American Citizenship* contains relevant "action projects" at the end of each chapter whose content neglects the historical context.[47] Gillespie and Lazarus, though generally better in discussing the historical context of an issue, have a section on "valuing" which treats values in an historical vacuum. After briefly discussing the history of the American labor movement, for instance, students are asked whether "the actions of John L. Lewis during the years 1920–1950 were *desirable* (emphasis added)."[48]

Another major improvement in civics textbook content—the decrease in the frequency of racial, ethnic, and cultural biases previously present in texts—may unintentionally have created its own problem. The increasing emphasis in civics textbooks on the multiracial, multicultural history of American social and political life, resulting from a concern over textbook bias, may have made it more difficult to draw out a common history and common values which are so crucial to democratic political community.[49]

Perhaps more important than the content of civics texts is the approach taken toward them in the classroom. Studies of American high school classrooms have shown that the textbook tends to be relied on exclusively and given complete authority as a source of knowledge. Students spend much of their classroom and homework time reading and memorizing the "civics gospel."[50] Teachers tend to reinforce this literal approach to texts in their class presentations and questions, and more importantly on exams, all of which have been found to assess the student's memory rather than her or his ability to read and think critically.[51] Fitzgerald contends that students generally "have to read all of each textbook and are rarely asked to criticize it for style or point of view. A textbook is there, much like Mount Everest awaiting George Mallory, and it leaves no alternative."[52]

Many of the textbooks reinforce a passive approach to reading their material. *Magruder's American Government* is notorious on this score, as it offers a "parade" of unchallenged institutional and historical facts. Whatever questions it includes that might encourage critical thought about textual material are buried at the end of a chapter and are overriden by the majority of questions which tend to assess *comprehension* of the readings rather than critical evaluation.

In this area, however, there have been some encouraging developments in the past few years. A number of texts now stress student "inquiry" and "participation in the learning process." Scholastic's *American Citizenship*, though weak in historical content (as seen above), pauses constantly in its narrative to get students to think critically about political practices and about the purposes of government. This stress on critical reading is reinforced by projects which require outside reading, observation, and research, and by such exercises as role-playing and group decision-making.[53]

Still, most texts tend to encourage a passive approach to reading which is antithetical to the building of citizenship skills or character. Democracy demands citizens who can evaluate critically the information and arguments they are given, in order to make decisions and solve problems in the public realm. To develop the kind of cognitive skills democratic citizens need, teachers must encourage students to take an active, confrontational attitude toward what they read. Locke put it this way: "In the books they read, students must stand to examine and unravel every argument and follow it step by step up to its original. . . . Reading furnishes the mind only with materials of knowledge; it is thinking makes what we read ours."[54]

There are a number of classroom methods which can be used to foster a more critical and active student stance toward civics texts. First, teachers can abandon the single textbook in favor of a multiplicity of reading sources. In government and history courses, teachers can use texts with differing views or emphases, or at least supplement the major text with other books, pamphlets, newspapers, and magazines, or even novels and plays. This kind of approach is beginning to have credence among secondary school educators.[55] A multiplicity of instructional materials can dissolve the external authority of a single text and make students themselves responsible for actively synthesizing the material they read.

Second, general classroom method can stimulate students' critical reading abilities. More will be said later on methods of instruction, but a more contentious and participatory classroom environment is likely to bring out a participatory attitude toward instructional materials. Classroom discussions involving controversial public issues are probably the best environment for teaching critical reading and thinking. A controversial classroom atmosphere not only tends to divest the textbook of its unchallenged authority, but may also motivate students to evaluate actively the information they are given, on the way to arriving at their own decisions about particular political issues or questions. In addition, a participatory component to the curriculum in general will help arouse students from their former passivity toward texts and other sources of information.

Of course, a paradox is involved here, for critical reading and contentious classroom discussions may instill in students a belief that all political principles and values are relative. Such a classroom atmosphere may foster students who are subjectivists rather than critical yet attached citizens committed to certain shared values. Nevertheless, it seems likely that by changing the content of civics texts in the ways described above—including more of the conflict and contention that make up the history of American politics as well as providing a greater background in intellectual history—and by changing our attitudes toward the textbook and its proper function in the classroom, we can better integrate instructional materials into an overall curriculum meant to develop the kinds of citizenship skills and attitudes suggested by the liberal and the participatory-republican conceptions.

The Broader Curriculum of Democratic Citizenship

Our two conceptions of democratic citizenship and citizenship education have suggested ways in which the social studies curriculum and its instructional materials could be made more conducive to the education of future democrats. But while the social studies curriculum is a good place to begin to address the contemporary problem of citizenship training in America, it will not do to end there. If we are serious about developing men and women capable of the wide range of skills and attitudes necessary for participation in democratic political life, we must move beyond a concern with government or civics courses proper, to an examination of the impact of the *entire* curriculum on citizen education.

Plato, in his discussion of the cycle of decay among cities, blames an imbalanced education in part for the degeneration of citizen character. One reason, he argues, that the "timocratic man" is less than ideal as a citizen is that he placed more value and time in his education on gymnastic than on music or dialectic. Similarly, "oligarchic" and "democratic" men have an imbalance in the training of their reason and desires, since not enough time was spent developing their rational faculties, so that their desires inordinately direct their public activity. The tyrant's character, Plato continues, is completely imbalanced and immoderate, his education taken over completely by the most base desires and dreams to the detriment of rational or intellectual capacities.[56] One contemporary educator has argued that the Greek educational aim was the pursuit of excellence in "autonomous action" and that the citizen's aim was "to become an effective speaker of words and doer of deeds in the polity of one's peers." The kind of civic involvement the Greeks aimed at required engaged but unspecialized individuals, who in turn required the most broadly based, integrated course of study possible. Only such a "general education" can empower "autonomous particulars to think critically about the full range of human activity and to judge soundly any and all efforts at action."[57]

Some contemporary educators have taken up the call for a broader conception of the civics curriculum. As we saw above, Fred Newmann and associates, though they do not go very far in integrating a wide range of disciplines into their civics program, do incorporate literature into their curricular scheme. Their "action in literature" course is meant to help students, through the reading of fiction, plays, and poetry, "to discuss concrete personal experiences of self and others in ways that contribute to the resolution of personal dilemmas encountered in civic action and that relate these experiences to more general human issues."[58] In addition, several professional educational societies have recently drawn up and circulated a statement entitled "Organizations for the Essentials of Education" which rejects simplistic solutions such as "back-to-basics" or "minimal competency testing" and instead argues for a more integrated curriculum as the most appropriate way of educating future democratic citizens:

> The overarching goal of education is to develop informed, thinking citizens capable of participating in both domestic and world affairs. The development of such citizens depends not only upon education for citizenship, but also upon other essentials of education shared by all subjects.[59]

Most recently, the Carnegie Foundation's report on secondary education echoes this concern for a broad core curriculum conducive to civic learning.

Some educators, then, have come to the realization that the social studies are not the only agent of citizen education. After a long period of specialized instruction, they are beginning to understand once again that many of the analytical and reasoning skills essential to good citizenship are better taught outside the social studies, in areas such as science and mathematics. Furthermore, the moral education that undergirds democratic political life requires an awareness that *all* disciplines contribute to our understanding of community values and how they have developed over time. But while general concern with a total curriculum for citizenship is growing, the particulars have not yet been addressed. We need to look back to earlier political and educational thinkers to explore what might make up a total curriculum for the education of citizens.

Mathematics and science instruction can teach skills and lessons appropriate to both the liberal and participatory-republican conceptions of democratic citizenship. Since the ability to reason critically—to analyze the connections between events, policies, or principles, and to move from abstract principles to concrete actions or policies and from concrete interests to more general laws and policies—is necessary under both conceptions of citizenship, a rigorous training in mathematics (specifically geometry and algebra) should make up a part of any citizen's complete education. For John Locke, mathematics was the best discipline of study for attaining general reasoning ability, as it accustoms the student to see the connections between things. Only by studying "mathematical demonstrations," said Locke, could a student aptly follow the "long train of consequences" that usually makes up political history and reasoning, as well as other parts of life and business.[60] Similarly, while Rousseau was willing to discard most other formal curricula for his fictional student Emile, he believed geometry to be a worthwhile way of providing a rational basis for the moral judgments a person would make throughout his or her life. For Rousseau, the student's progress in geometry could serve as a "certain measure of the development of his intelligence."[61]

Study in the sciences has also been justified in terms of its benefits to citizen education. Charles Eliot wanted science to be one of the primary components of a universal public education, since it enables students to "acquire a capacity for exact observation" and gives them "the power to draw a justly limited inference from observed facts." In fact, said Eliot, a democratic politics depended upon instilling a scientific understanding in each citizen: "Democratic institutions will not be safe until a great majority of the population can be trusted not only to observe accurately and state precisely the results of observation, but also to draw just inferences from those results."[62] Israel Scheffler, a contemporary "liberal" educator, argues that the connection between scientific and democratic education lies in the perspective of reasonableness at the heart of both. Education in science, he says, can teach students to question, to scrutinize the evidence behind particular arguments, and to judge critically what is presented to them; thus it cultivates the kind of "reasonableness" needed by democratic citizens.[63]

It can be argued, then, that closer attention should be paid to the positive effects of science and mathematics on the education of democratic citizens, as training in both disciplines develops the cognitive reasoning skills essential to citizenship as well as better preparing citizens for more active participation in the public discussion of matters involving scientific understanding. A better integration of art and literature into an entire "civics" curriculum can also be argued for, since education in these areas not only provides vicarious concrete experience (as argued above), but also leads to the development and application of standards of taste and judgment in ways similar to the development of political values and standards.

Music education may also be important to democratic citizens, especially under the participatory-republican conception. Plato argued that education in music is important because it brings a sense of rhythm and harmony to the soul which makes individuals more moderate in their desires and better judges in matters of both private and public taste. In addition, Plato felt that the metaphor of musical harmony is one that carries over into relations among fellow citizens, with musical sensibility helping create bonds of cooperation between people living together in the political community.[64] An education in music may help develop the psychological character traits which participatory-republicans feel are basic to social and political relations among men and women.[65]

This discussion only suggests different areas of study with which an integrated curriculum should be concerned. In order to get an idea of just how a total civics curriculum which incorporates various disciplines in the service of citizen education might look, we will concentrate on three different thinkers' visions of such curriculum: the visions of Benjamin Rush, Antonio Gramsci, and John Dewey. Though all three had somewhat different goals in mind, all fall within what this study would consider to be the participatory-republican conception of democratic citizenship. With these three we can get a better idea of how a revitalization of the participatory-republican conception of citizenship would infuse our current curricula with democratic energy.

Benjamin Rush, writing in the early days of the American republic, articulated what he considered to be the proper "total" curriculum for citizens in a republic. Rush, like other republican thinkers, placed a heavy emphasis on the study of history, "the art of war," and "practical legislation" as key elements in civic training. But Rush was also intent on establishing a rigorous study of "the language of our country," which would include the "study of eloquence." This he considered essential to the civics curriculum since he believed that the development of powers of eloquence in each citizen is "the first accomplishment in a republic and often sets the whole machine of government in motion."[66] Rush's "republican curriculum" also included "vocal music," which he felt "civiliz[es] the mind and thereby prepar[es] it for the influence of religion and government"; intervals of manual labor mixed with those of study, to inculcate habits of industry, humility, association, and discipline; and even a proper and "temperate diet," which he felt would not only develop healthy citizens but would also teach the psychological lessons of moderation and self-discipline that make up a part of the republican conception of citizen character.[67] Finally, Rush wanted Christian religion to be taught as part of the public school curriculum. Unlike those who were against "filling the minds of youth with religious prejudices" and desired that "they should be left to choose their own principles after they have arrived at an age in which they are capable of judging for themselves," Rush believed that children would run into religious principles in an unorganized way throughout childhood, and that instruction in religion would not only prepare them for free inquiry into the religion of their choice, but would be conducive to the creation of republican values in citizens: "A Christian cannot fail of being a republican for every precept of the gospel inculcates those degrees of humility, self-denial, and brotherly kindness which are directly opposed to the pride of a monarchy and the pageantry of a court." Christianity he believed to be also conducive to republican political association and collective political action, since it teaches people "that no man liveth unto himself."[68] Through this diverse but connected curriculum, Rush attempted not only to teach the practical and cognitive skills necessary to citizen participation in republican politics, but also to develop the psychological and affective dispositions appropriate to a participatory-republican politics.

Though writing in a different country in the twentieth century, Antonio Gramsci also considered the effects of the entire curriculum in the development of a democratic consciousness in citizens. The kind of well-rounded curriculum Gramsci proposed for developing democratic citizens would be "disinterested" and without "immediate or too immediate practical purposes."[69] A true civics curriculum, according to Gramsci, should emphasize the traditional disciplines of grammar, "descriptive philosophy" and logic, the study of classical languages, and mathematics, in addition to the social studies disciplines of history and law. Gramsci proposed "the grammatical study of Latin and Greek" as a means of producing the kind of "disinterestedness" characteristic of the democratic personality:

> The real interest [of such study] was the interior development of personality, by means of the absorption and assimilation of the whole cultural past of modern European civilisation. Pupils did not learn Latin and Greek in order to speak them, to become waiters, interpreters or commercial letter writers. They learnt them in order to know at first hand the civilisation of Greece and Rome—a civilisation that was a necessary precondition of our modern civilisation: in other words, they learnt them in order to be themselves and know themselves consciously.[70]

The study of languages such as Latin and Greek, he said, not only develops "disinterestedness," but also fulfills a series of "pedagogical and psychological requirements" of democratic citizenship. Gramsci believed these languages also should be studied in order to accustom children to studying in a specific manner, and to analysing an historical body which can be treated as a corpse which continually returns to life; in order to accustom them to reason, to think abstractly and schematically while remaining able to plunge back from abstraction into real and immediate life, to see in each fact or datum what is general and what is particular, to distinguish the concept from the specific instance.[71]

Gramsci also included philosophy, mathematics, and the rigorous study of grammar as elements of an integrated course of study for future citizens, since he felt that they developed in the student a kind of "formal logic" which could be "assimilated in a living way" into civic discourse. When one adds these traditional disciplines to a course of social studies which teaches "rights and duties" and "the notions of the state and society as primordial elements of a new conception of the world" going beyond individual or family, one gets Gramsci's conception of the most adequate preparation for democratic life.[72]

The importance for Gramsci of teaching indirectly political subjects in conjunction with the "standard" civics program in history and government is clear. Gramsci held that only through these "non-political subjects" could one "inculcate certain habits of diligence, precision, poise, the ability to concentrate on specific subjects, which cannot be acquired without the mechanical repetition of disciplined and methodical acts," all of which are involved in courses of grammar, logic, and mathematics.[73] He believed that this kind of integrated curriculum would produce the kind of self-discipline and self-control necessary to democratic self-governance and an autonomous yet cooperative politics. The "disinterested" nature of such a curriculum, according to Gramsci, would begin to teach the student the "disinterestedness" characteristic of laws and policies that result from a democratic decision-making process. Gramsci opposed the educational reforms proposed by other Italian leftists, which called for greater student leeway in the choice of courses and a more practical or vocational program of study, because he felt these had the "tendency to ease off the discipline of studies, and to ask for 'relaxations.'"[74] Gramsci felt this more "vocational" or "elective" education was profoundly anti-democratic in reality, while appearing on the surface to be democratic, appealing to individual student "interests." Instead, his integrated curriculum was meant to provide a rigorous universal education for all students as a preparation for universal political participation.

John Dewey also saw a broad-based curriculum as the best means of preparing citizens in the skills and values necessary to democratic political life. For Dewey, the student's experience was a single whole; it was a mistake to divide and classify the curriculum into separate subjects which rarely interpenetrate. Dewey's "civics program" consisted of courses in mathematics and geometry, to develop abstract reasoning skills; in science, to develop "concrete reasoning" ability and observation skills; in history, to inculcate in the student what Dewey calls "social reasoning"; in foreign languages, which aid in the development of memory (Dewey felt this was crucial for a democracy, where people's memories of the past are important to their proper judging and ruling on present and future policies); in English literature, to "hone" a student's skills in judgment, taste, and evaluation of standards; and in poetry (especially Greek and Latin poetry) and writing, to develop the student's imagination and ability to express him- or herself clearly and forcefully (which, as we saw earlier in this chapter, is crucial to democratic discussion and debate). Like Rush and Gramsci, Dewey felt that by creating an integrated course of study the schools could develop well-rounded citizens possessing all the cognitive skills and attitudes essential to participation in a democratic society.[75]

These thinkers' notions of a proper civics curriculum are not presented here as a blueprint for secondary schools today. The three men were writing in different times and places, and were responding to somewhat different circumstances. Nonetheless, their ideas about the curriculum appropriate to citizenship education should be considered seriously, since they illustrate the importance of having a more integrated civics program incorporating more than the traditional social studies fare typical of most contemporary secondary schools. These thinkers realized that instruction in science, mathematics, literature, languages, art, and even music is critical to developing both the cognitive skills and affective attitudes that characterize democratic citizens. They understood that only by thinking about the impact of the *total* curriculum on the creation of citizen character can all of the attributes of citizenship be properly developed in conjunction with each other and brought together in the well-rounded democratic citizen. High school educators can learn from these thinkers that a better civic training for their students stems from a more integrated approach to the curriculum. Those concerned about the education of citizens must recognize that it is fruitless to concentrate on individual civics or social studies courses, since "from the student's point of view schooling is a synthesis of many experiences, not a collection of isolated encounters with particular teachers or subjects."[76]

NOTES

1. Robert Barr, James L. Barth, and S. Samuel Shermis, *Defining the Social Studies* (National Council for the Social Studies, 1977) 19–20.

2. Rolla Tryon, *The Social Sciences as School Subjects, Part XI: Report of the Commission on Social Studies* (New York: Charles Scribner's Sons, 1935), 176; see also National Education Association, *Report of the Committee of Ten on Secondary School Subjects* (Washington: U.S. Bureau of Education, 1892), 190.

3. Barr, et al., *Defining the Social Studies,* 22–28.

4. Ibid., 39–42.

5. Jerome Bruner's classic *The Process of Education* (Cambridge: Harvard University Press, 1960) is considered by many to be the major influence here. Typical of the "separate social science disciplines" approach was the publication of the influential *Concepts and Structures in the New Social Studies Curriculum,* by the Social Science Educational Consortium (Irving Morrissett, ed., Chicago: Holt, Rinehart and Winston, 1967), in which a leading scholar from each separate discipline would lay out the conceptual approach to his or her subject's study, with little overlapping between disciplines.

6. National Council for the Social Studies, *The Social Studies and the Social Sciences* (New York: Harcourt Brace and World, 1962), 6–7.

7. Barr, et al., *Defining the Social Studies,* 63.

8. However, a 1969 ETS survey of the teaching of history and social studies in the secondary schools concluded that the organization and content of courses had not changed significantly over the previous twenty-five years, indicating that the New Social Studies may never really have been implemented in its "true spirit" in the high schools; see Elisabeth G. Kimball, *A Survey of the Teaching of History and Social Studies in Secondary Schools* (Princeton: Educational Testing Service, 1969), 3–4.

9. See Edwin Fenton, *Teaching the New Social Studies in Secondary Schools* (New

York: Holt, Rinehart, Winston, 1966). See also Frances Fitzgerald's discussion of Fenton in *America Revised*, 183–88.

10. Sidney Simon, "Values Clarification vs. Indoctrination," in Simon, *Values Concepts and Techniques* (Washington: National Education Association, 1976), 135.

11. Simon, "Values Clarification," 135–43; see also Louis Raths, Merrill Harmon, and Sidney Simon, *Values and Teaching* (Columbus, Ohio: Merrill, 1966).

12. See Andrew Oldenquist, "On the Nature of Citizenship," *Educational Leadership* (October 1980): pp. 30–33.

13. Lawrence Kohlberg, "Stage and Sequence: The Cognitive-Developmental Approach to Socialization," in David Goslin, ed., *Handbook of Socialization Theory and Research* (Chicago: Rand-McNally and Co., 1969), 347–80. See also Edwin Fenton, "The Implications of Lawrence Kohlberg's Research for Civic Education," in *Education for Responsible Citizenship*, 97–132.

14. Fenton, Ibid., 107–9.

15. In a sample of 2400 Illinois high school students, a majority said that civics courses did not increase their interest in government, public affairs, or politics (Illinois State Office of Education, *Illinois Inventory of Educational Progress: Citizenship Curricular Analyses and Teacher Expectation Results* [Washington: ERIC, June 1980]). Langton and Jennings's landmark socialization study in the late 1960s also found few positive changes in most students' political knowledge, information, efficacy, interest, or civic tolerance after taking high school civics courses; Kenneth Langton and M. Kent Jennings, "Political Socialization and the High School Civics Curriculum in the U.S.," *American Political Science Review* (September 1968): 852–67.

16. Judith Torney, et al., *Civic Education in Ten Countries* (New York: John Wiley and Sons, 1975), 327–35.

17. Silberman, *Crisis in the Classroom*, 183.

18. See, among others, James Shaver, "A Critical View of the Social Studies Profession," *Social Education* (April 1977): 300–09. This lack of integration is also made manifest by the proliferation of specialized education journals, separated by both subject-matter and level of instruction.

19. Phillip Jackson, "Comprehending a Well-Run Comprehensive: A Report on a Visit to a Large Suburban High School," *Daedalus* (Fall 1981): 86–89. This is a major criticism of the Carnegie Foundation's report; see Boyer, *High School*, 71–117.

20. Dewey, *Democracy and Education*, 249.

21. Ibid., 163. See also Alfred North Whitehead, *The Aims of Education* (New York: MacMillan, 1929), for a similar argument.

22. See Arthur Bestor, *The Restoration of Learning* (New York: Alfred A. Knopf, 1956), 126ff.

23. Rousseau, *Emile*, 237.

24. Ibid., 237.

25. Thomas Jefferson, "Notes on the State of Virginia, Query XIV," in *Portable Jefferson*, 198.

26. S. M. Shumer, "Republican Politics," 25.

27. Locke, *Some Thoughts Concerning Education*, 146–48.

28. Stephen Bailey, "Political and Social Purposes of Education," in *Education for Responsible Citizenship*, 39–40.

29. See Newmann, et al., *Skills in Citizen Action*.

30. In Silberman, *Crisis in the Classroom*, 173.

31. The NSF study results are discussed in James Shaver, et al., "The Status of

Social Studies Education: Impressions From Three NSF Studies," *Social Education* (February 1979): 150–53.

32. *Magruder's American Government*, revised by William McClenaghan (Boston: Allyn and Bacon, 1981).

33. Ibid., preface.

34. Roberta Sigel, "Students' Comprehension of Democracy and Its Application to Conflict Situations," *International Journal of Political Education* 2 (1979): 48.

35. McClenaghan, *Magruder's American Government*, 26.

36. John Patrick and Richard Remy, *Civics for Americans* (New York: Scott, Foresman, 1980).

37. The five texts are Richard Gross, *American Citizenship: The Way We Govern*, (Addison-Wesley Publishing Company, 1979); Judith Gillespie and Stuart Lazarus, *American Government: Comparing Political Experiences*, (Englewood Cliffs, New Jersey: Prentice-Hall, 1979); Alan O. Kownslar and Terry L. Smart, *American Government* (New York: McGraw-Hill, 1980); Armin Rosencranz and James B. Chapin, *American Government* (New York: Holt, Rinehart, and Winston, 1979); *Scholastic American Citizenship*, revised edition (New York: Scholastic Book Services, 1980).

38. Rosencranz & Chapin, *American Government*. See introduction and teacher's guide.

39. Gross, *American Citizenship*, 280.

40. Fitzgerald, *America Revised*, 162.

41. Rosencranz & Chapin, *American Government*; see especially chapters 1, 13, 14, 19.

42. Lewis Paul Todd and Merle Curti, *Rise of the American Nation*, Heritage Edition (New York: Harcourt, Brace Jovanovich, 1977).

43. Fitzgerald, *America Revised*, 151–53.

44. McClenaghan, *Magruder's American Government*, 305, 209, 224, respectively.

45. Ibid., 61, 302, 491, respectively.

46. Gross, *American Citizenship*, 49.

47. See, for example, the Action Project on the Suez Canal, *Scholastic American Citizenship*, 764–65.

48. Gillespie and Lazarus, *American Government*, 164.

49. Fitzgerald makes this argument in *America Revised*, 104–05. She also contends that with the constant changes that occur in texts every few years, each generation of Americans is reading a history that is "transient" in its general tone, impression, and atmosphere. Each generation may emerge with a different understanding of history, which also creates problems for political community; see also 17–18.

50. A governor's commission on public education in Texas found that 75 percent of classroom time and 90 percent of homework time was spent on textbooks; see Paul Goldstein, *Changing the American Schoolbook* (Lexington: D. C. Heath and Co., 1978), 121.

51. One survey of secondary school social studies teachers showed that over 60 percent of the questions they asked in class about their students' reading materials fell into the "memory assessment" category, while less than 8 percent of the questions asked students to evaluate, analyze, apply, or synthesize the material read; see John Godbold, "Oral Questioning Practices of Teachers in Social Studies Classes," *Educational Leadership* (1970): 61–67. Another study testing items on social studies exams in high schools revealed that less than 10 percent assessed critical reading skills or could be considered relevant to critical thinking; see John Popenfus and Louis Para-

dise, "Social Studies Objectives in Theory and Practice," *The Social Studies* 69 (1978): 200–03.

52. Fitzgerald, *America Revised,* 27.

53. Gross, *American Citizenship,* and Gillespie and Lazarus, *American Government,* are also very good on this score.

54. Locke, *Of the Conduct of the Understanding,* 73–75.

55. For example, see the issue in *Social Education* (February 1980) on approaches to social studies textbooks.

56. Plato, *The Republic of Plato,* ed. Allan Bloom (New York: Basic Books, 1968), books 7–9.

57. Robert McClintock, "The Dynamics of Decline: Why Education Can No Longer Be Liberal," *Phi Delta Kappan* (May 1979): 636–40.

58. Newmann, et al., *Skills in Citizen Action,* 74.

59. Quoted by R. Freeman Butts in "Curriculum for the Educated Citizen," *Educational Leadership* (October 1980): 6.

60. Locke, *Of the Conduct,* 51–55; *Some Thoughts,* 143–45, 160–61.

61. Rousseau, *Emile,* 167.

62. Charles W. Eliot, "The Function of Education in a Democratic Society," in Eliot, *Educational Reform: Essays and Addresses* (New York: Century Co., 1898), 410–11. John Dewey felt that without an education for all in science and the scientific method, an expertise and technical specialization could easily develop, antithetical to citizens democratically making decisions based upon scientific understanding and observation. See Dewey, *Democracy and Education,* 286–88.

63. Israel Scheffler, "Moral Education and the Democratic Ideal," in Scheffler, *Reason and Teaching* (London: Routledge and Kegan Paul, 1973), 142–44.

64. Plato, *Republic* 80–89.

65. Locke was opposed to the study of music as a part of the young man's overall education, since "it wastes so much of a young man's time." He comments, "I have, amongst men of parts and business, so seldom heard any one commended or esteemed for having excellency in music, that amongst all those things, that ever came into the list of accomplishments, I think I may give it the last place." Locke, *Some Thoughts Concerning Education,* 162–63.

66. Benjamin Rush, "Thoughts Upon the Mode of Education Proper in a Republic," in Rudolph, ed., *Essays on Education in the Early Republic* (Cambridge: Harvard University Press, 1965), 18–19.

67. Ibid., 15.

68. Ibid., 11.

69. Antonio Gramsci, "On Education," *Selections From the Prison Notebooks,* ed. Quintin Hoare and Geoffrey Smith (New York: International Publishers, 1971), 40.

70. Ibid., 37.

71. Ibid., 38.

72. Ibid., 30, 42.

73. Ibid., 37.

74. Ibid., 42.

75. Dewey, *Democracy and Education,* 152–53, 243–45.

76. Richard Merelman, "Democratic Politics and the Culture of American Education," *American Political Science Review* 74, no. 2 (June 1980): 319.

CHAPTER 5

The Implicit Curriculum
of the Democratic Citizen

W E HAVE JUST EXAMINED the relationship between formal, explicit curricula and the teaching of citizenship norms and skills in secondary schools. But the kind of "overt" curriculum which we have been discussing does not constitute the entire picture of what is learned in high schools. Many educational writers have described the real presence of what has been called a "hidden curriculum," whose lessons are not only detrimental to the student's education in general but are particularly destructive to efforts in *democratic* citizen education. It may even be, as Edgar Friedenberg has argued, that "what is learned in high school . . . depends far less on what is taught than on what one actually experiences in the place." For many, in terms of civic education, these are two different things, due to the hidden curriculum.[1]

The hidden curriculum arises out of the school's organizational imperative that there be order, hierarchical control, efficiency, and organized competition among students. Due to their concern with order, schools tend to organize tight time schedules, teach students submission to their teachers' control in classrooms, group students according to "ability," and closely supervise all school activity.[2] Teachers are advised to reinforce the school's order and control constantly, by placing primary concern on discipline and orderly movement as well as by avoiding explosive topics of discussion or learning. A piece of advice given to teachers by the National Education Association in the late 1960s illustrates this concern:

Avoid standing with your back to the class for any length of time. If you do, you may invite disorderly conduct. . . . Avoid emotion-charged topics. Discussing them may lead to an argument so explosive that fighting can result. Until a group has achieved enough maturity to keep itself under control, it is better to risk boredom than pandemonium.[3]

The hidden curriculum tends to produce an "authoritarian atmosphere"[4] under which all formal lessons are learned, teaching the student not only algebra but also passivity, not only physics but also the need for constant submission to teachers, not only government but also inordinate dependency, not only music but also orderly competition among and inequality between students. The hidden curriculum has serious implications for the education of democratic citizens in America. Charles Silberman contends that because of the presence of the hidden curriculum,

far from helping students to develop into mature, self-reliant, self-motivated individuals, schools seem to do everything they can to keep youngsters in a state of chronic, almost infantile, dependency. The pervasive atmosphere of distrust, together with rules covering the most minute aspects of existence, teach students every day that they are not people of worth, and certainly not individuals capable of regulating their own behavior.[5]

Richard Merelman summarizes the argument about the hidden curriculum by saying that "students cannot learn democracy in the school because the school is not a democratic place."[6]

The presence of a hidden curriculum in high schools is severely disruptive to the political education of future democrats. Not only does the "authoritarian atmosphere" of order and discipline promote attitudes of passivity, unhealthy dependency, submission, competition, and inequality that may be transferred to the polity, but it also prevents the actual teaching of values essential to democratic political behavior. Merelman feels that the stressing of order and routine in the classroom often forces teachers to avoid conflictual discussions of political values, goals, ideas, and even particular governmental policies:

Teaching political values poses a threat to the delicate conjunction of order and content that makes up the basic shape of schooling. Discussing political values in the classroom invites controversy and division, especially in the United States where a heritage of liberalism encourages citizens to make unfettered political choices from a free market of ideas.[7]

Not feeling able to engage in lively intellectual exchange, teachers must resort either to ignoring political ideas, goals, and values altogether or to presenting certain "fundamental values" as facts not open to dispute. What often results from high school civics classes conducted in this manner is that students emerge with shallowly held democratic beliefs, since the fortitude of their beliefs has not been tested in the fire of conflict and controversy. The irony is that without allowing for any heated intellectual debate over political values or goals, schools are undermining one of the very foundations for order in a democratic setting—internalized consensus over fundamental values.

The presence of a hidden curriculum in the schools makes the inclusion of one additional element in the total civics curriculum crucial: participation. When a strong participatory component is included as an integral part of citizen education, both in and out of the classroom, students will learn important lessons in direct political decision-making, and can overcome most dangerous effects of the hidden curriculum more easily. Research findings have shown that students who have participatory experience, not only in classrooms that practice some type of "discovery method" of instruction or student decision-making about the direction courses should take, but also in broader school policies and activities, are more likely to exhibit "democratic" attributes. These students have been found to be more likely to be informed about how political decisions are reached and the alternative ways of reaching them, to have more self-confidence, and to be more actively "participatory" in motivation and more skillful in the art of weighing opinions, negotiating, dissenting, and discussing issues of mutual concern.[8]

Student participation as a part of the civics curriculum would also include involvement in organizations, projects, and activities outside the school in the community at large. The National Panel on High Schools and Adolescent Education in 1974 observed that classroom approaches to civics instruction had brought "little technical proficiency in closing the gap between classroom study and an active citizenship." The panel recommended that civic education be moved out into the community by involving students in social, political, and governmental agencies.[9] More recently, the Carnegie Foundation's report on secondary education in 1983 recommended that "every high school student complete a service requirement—a new 'Carnegie Unit'—involving volunteer work in the community or at school." The Commission saw student participation in community service as not only overcoming aspects of the hidden curriculum, but also helping students learn that they "are not only autonomous individuals but also members of a larger community to which they are accountable."[10]

Some schools have initiated programs involving students in community projects and direct community research, volunteer organizations, and government agencies and institutions. Educators involved with these programs feel that when students perform significant commmunity functions—having a say and a responsibility in them, working with others on common goals, and having others depend on their actions—their cognitive and affective knowledge, necessary to democratic citizenship, is enhanced more effectively than by classroom instruction alone. Through direct community participation, politics comes alive for students and begins to be defined as encompassing more than mere voting or what goes on in state and national capitals. Classroom knowledge becomes better integrated through students' community participation, as classroom lessons and ideals are linked to actions students undertake and reflect upon together. Classroom discussion about broad political issues and goals is also enhanced by direct participation. Furthermore, student participation may enliven and educate the community at large, and better integrate young student-citizens in common projects with people from different age groups and walks of life. (Keeping students in school full-time tends to isolate them from older generations and from the "real world" of the community around them.)[11]

Civic participation as a component of citizen education is especially important if we are to revive elements of the participatory-republican model of citizenship. Alexis de Tocqueville laid out most clearly the "republican" argument for participation in extracurricular associations as an educational device. After observing the function of civic associations in America, Tocqueville concluded that participation in both political and social associations was essential to maintaining democratic institutions and to educating people for citizenship. He argued that in democratic polities, "all the citizens are independent and feeble; they can do hardly anything by themselves, and none of them can oblige his fellow men to lend him their assistance. They all therefore become powerless if they do not learn voluntarily to help one another."[12] Participation in civic associations educates people to overcome this powerlessness and isolation, since through such participation members of associations learn "the art of pursuing in common the object of their common desires" and of "proposing a common object for the exertions of a great many men and inducing them voluntarily to pursue it."[13]

Tocqueville felt that only through membership in political and social associations can both the cognitive and affective attributes of citizens in a republic be developed: ". . . feelings and opinions are recruited, the heart is enlarged, and the human mind is developed only by the reciprocal influence of men upon one another."[14] Through participation in these associations, he said, "Americans of all conditions, minds, and ages, daily acquire a general taste for association and grow accustomed to the use of it. There they meet together in large numbers, they converse, they listen to one another, and they are stimulated to all sorts of undertakings."[15] Participation in various kinds of civic associations is therefore an important element of republican citizen education, with such associations or extracurricular civic projects serving as "large free schools," where students can learn "the general theory of association" as a part of the overall training to call forth in each citizen the "reflective patriotism of a republic."[16]

The participatory-republican conception certainly requires a participatory emphasis in the school curriculum. But participation also fits into the civics curriculum under the liberal conception of democratic citizenship. Though citizen participation does tend to be downplayed by contemporary liberal-democratic writers, it would still appear to have an important function in teaching future citizens how to secure their interests through at least minimal political participation. Participation is also useful in exposing students to the "rules of the game" and the social values which undergird liberal politics.

Furthermore, participation as a part of the curriculum of citizenship education can be epistemologically justified from both a liberal and a participatory-republican perspective. Participation provides students with direct *empirical* knowledge of political phenomena, and encourages further exploration both in and out of the classroom (corresponding to the empirical thrust in liberal thought about education). Moreover, participation provides opportunities for direct action with others to alter conditions in the political environment (the source of political knowledge and individual educational transformation under an "activist epistemology" characteristic of many participatory-republican thinkers).

Madness in Its Methods?

The preceding discussion of the "hidden curriculum" and its pernicious effects on the education of democratic citizens should alert us to the impact not only of the curriculum but of *methods of instruction* on citizen education. It may be that the subject matter of the civics curriculum, or *what* is taught explicitly, is less important to the traits and values learned in school than the method of instruction, or *how* a subject is taught.

Political theorists writing about education have long recognized the dual importance of educational content and method. John Locke felt that the method used to teach children was as important as the substantive content taught to them. Since he felt that "the business of education . . . is not as I think, to make the young perfect in any one of the sciences, but so to open and dispose their minds as may best make them capable of any, when they shall apply themselves to it,"[17] Locke maintained that it was necessary to choose a mode of instruction conducive to opening young minds to all future educational encounters. For Rousseau, teaching method was more important than the formal curriculum of studies, since he considered the student's educational independence and psychological predispositions toward learning to be the essence of education, rather than the quantity of "educational truths" learned. Rousseau held that in education "the goal is less to teach [the student] a truth than to show him how he must go about discovering the truth."[18]

The need to consider curriculum and method jointly is particularly pressing in the area of citizen education. The method and process of learning to be good democratic citizens cannot be separated from the actual subject matter taught, or democratic experiences acquired, since as we saw when examining the hidden curriculum it is difficult to learn the principles of democracy in a profoundly undemocratic setting. And given the contingencies of decision-making in a participatory democracy, future citizens are poorly served by a civics curriculum that is fixed in content and rigidly inculcated. The fact that in a democratic polity there may be no absolute truths, but only policies and decisions agreed upon to deal with fluid and contingent political situations, makes it imperative, as Locke and Rousseau argued, that students be taught in such a way that they have the foundations to know what procedures to engage in to find "political truths" with their fellow citizens. They must also be taught in a way that encourages intellectual openness and a belief in their own dignity and in the powers of their political understanding. A democratic civics curriculum must seek not only to integrate individual subjects, as maintained above, but also to integrate subject matter and method.

Contemporary American educators tend to pay little attention to the impact of teaching methods on the education of citizens. They tend to focus on the actual curricular content of civics classes—the kinds of texts used and projects or programs outside the classroom—but rarely look at the impact on citizen education of the method of teaching in the social studies classroom. In fact, the National Commission on the Reform of Secondary Education's report cited above concludes that methods of instruction are not important to learning in secondary schools:

> The sources of educational experiences are relatively unimportant; what matters is whether or not they deliver the knowledge and skills required by learners. . . . The degree to which goals are achieved, *not the manner of instruction,* should be the basis on which the effectiveness of a school is assessed (emphasis added).[19]

But the methods with which we teach citizen skills and values are not as unimportant or as neutral as many modern educators claim. Indeed, setting aside the organizational imperatives of schools (the hidden curriculum), the major methods employed in high school classes today are *detrimental* in important ways to the teaching of democratic norms.

The main manner of instruction in the past was what has alternately been called the "vertical cultural transmission model,"[20] the "static, cold-storage ideal of knowledge,"[21] and the "banking concept of education"[22] by various twentieth-century critics. Knowledge was seen as "inert" and "encyclopedic," to be transmitted by "old, mature and experienced teachers" to "young, immature and inexperienced pupils."[23] Since all lessons, including those of citizenship, were intended to bring about "the accumulation and acquisition of information for purposes of reproduction in recitation and examination,"[24] students were seen as "receptacles to be stuffed full of empirical data and a mass of unconnected raw facts" by teachers.[25] While a continuing revolt begun by progressives at the turn of the century has overturned much of the thrust of this "vertical transmission" method of teaching, the characteristics of the hidden curriculum which pervade most secondary schools prove that the "top-down," subject-centered (as opposed to child-centered) approach still exists today.[26] And a Harvard School of Education study of the school system of "Watertown," Massachusetts in the late 1960s shockingly demonstrates the presence of a commitment to this method of instruction in contemporary times:

> Watertown's schools do not give the student many opportunities to assume responsibility for his own learning. . . . The pervasive method of instruction consists of lectures and teacher-dominated activities. The teacher talks; the students are expected to listen or recite in response to the teacher's cues. The emphasis is on the acquisition of factual information untempered by reflective thought. Textbooks determine course content and organization, and many courses are untouched by current thought in curricular development. In Watertown, the student succeeds by being quiet, by following directions, and by memorizing the information which the teacher doles out. The teacher succeeds by following textbook instructions.[27]

This hierarchical method of conveying the subject-matter of citizen education clearly collides with goals of democratic politics. As we observed in our discussion of the hidden curriculum, the "banking concept of education" is likely to create student passivity and submission rather than the active participation and critical awareness essential to democratic citizenship. Dewey felt that under this method of purely "mechanical learning," the student's

> seeming attention, his docility, his memorizing and reproductions, will partake of intellectual servility. Such a condition of intellectual subjection is needed for fitting the masses into a society where the many are not expected to have aims or ideas of their own, but to take orders from the few set in authority. It is not adapted to a society which intends to be democratic.[28]

But the student not only fails to develop the democratic behavioral and attitudinal attributes of self-reliance, autonomy, critical thinking, and self-discipline; he or she is also less likely to be knowledgeable about politics under a rigid, one-way method of instruction. Dewey also argued that a disciplinary, hierarchical approach to education ultimately fails to incite sufficient interest in the school's subject matter: "[Under a "disciplinary" method], the subject matter does not appeal; it cannot appeal; it lacks origin and bearing in a growing experience."[29] Democratic citizenship, therefore, requires some degree of dialogue and individual student participation in the educational process.

If, however, the traditional, subject-centered, "vertical-transmission" method of teaching civics comes into severe conflict with the stated objectives and content of democratic citizenship education, so too does its major contemporary alternative, the child-centered or individualized instruction method. Influenced by Dewey and the progressive movement in education as well as by Freudian psychology, educators in this century began to come to "the opinion that the child, not the subject of study, is the guide to the teacher's efforts."[30] This emphasis on paying primary attention to the child's educational interests and his or her autonomy in the learning process, initiated by some progressives, has now ballooned (spurred on by the reaction against the subject-centeredness and authoritarian nature of the "social science disciplines" approach mentioned above) into proposals and programs for *completely* individualized instruction. Many contemporary educators have come to feel that, as far as the curriculum is concerned,

> the individual is central; the individual in the deepest sense, *is* the culture, not the institution (of the school). His culture resides in him,

in experience and memory, and what is needed is an education that has as its base the sanctity of the individual's experience *and leaves it intact* (emphasis added).[31]

As we mentioned earlier, the National Commission for the Reform of Secondary Education moved completely away from any notion of "common" schools, proposing instead the "provision of basically different means, perhaps even different ends, for the individual student." This complete individualization of instruction would accomplish the Commission's desired goal of "fitting the school to the student, providing him with meaningful options for his own style of learning in the context of his own aspirations."[32] In response to the call for a more "child-centered curriculum," alternative educational structures have sprung up (some of whose impact on citizenship education we will discuss in the next chapter), to the point that some educators and communications specialists talk about total individualization of instruction through computer- and television-assisted education.[33]

An overly child-centered curriculum has a number of pernicious effects on democratic citizenship education. Psychologically, a completely individualized instruction may accustom students to always getting their way, their particular educational whims having dominion over the teacher and the rest of the school. A child-centered pedagogy will not incline individual students to see themselves as just one of a group of equally deserving students in whose presence they must limit their particular desires and share educational time and resources, to learn the participatory-republican's lessons of humility, interdependence, and the need to put reason and desires in equilibrium. Neither will it teach the individual student the liberal psychological lessons of deference to others and to social rules and customs, what Mill called "the habit . . . of subordinating [one's] personal impulses and aims to what were considered the ends of society."[34] Thus, an educational method which "has at its base the sanctity of the individual's experience and leaves it intact" is contrary to *both* the liberal and the participatory-republican conceptions of citizen education, since both society for the liberal and the political community for the participatory-republican require that the individual moderate his or her particular impulses and become an other-regarding actor.

A method which individualizes instruction to the extent proposed by many contemporary educational reformers misses another central part of citizen education under the participatory-republican conception. For participatory-republicans, the idea of structuring a curriculum around the needs and interests of each individual student, and leaving the student to his or her own program, forgets that "the child's consciousness is not something *individual*."[35] Dewey felt that the trend toward a one-sided absorption in individual students, yielding to their interests and attempting only to increase their specialized abilities, ultimately neglects the social environment which gives any learning *meaning* and *application*:

> When treating [education] as a separate conscious business of this sort tends to preclude the social sense which comes from sharing in an activity of common concern and value, the effort at isolated intellectual learning contradicts its aim. . . . Only by engaging in a joint activity, where one person's use of material and tools is consciously referred to the use other persons are making of their capacities and appliances, is a social direction of disposition attained.[36]

Instead of providing a context in which students of different backgrounds and interests come together to share educational experiences and discuss their different views on various subjects, schools today propagate methods which, in one observer's eyes, have led to "the gradual emergence of an educational environment in which the importance of individual differences is magnified."[37] While methods of individualized instruction have overturned obsolete methods based upon the "vertical transmission" of knowledge, they have not created forms of "lateral transmission" appropriate to participatory democratic politics. A method of individualized instruction divides the "community" of the classroom, at best providing relationships based upon comparison and competition among students.

The more extreme forms of individualized instruction, which use the television and computer as teaching devices, not only tend to mold the students into passive spectators, reactors to the stimuli presented (therefore perpetuating student nonparticipation), but also fail to provide the kind of interaction through reasoned speech and dialogue, with fellow students and the teacher, that symbolizes the sharing and deliberation with others characteristic of relations between citizens in a democracy. From a participatory-republican perspective, at least, the individualized tutorial relationship between student and teacher (or a television or a computer) that develops out of a child-centered method of instruction can never serve the political ends of citizen education.

A method of citizenship education conducive to participatory-republican conceptions of citizenship would incorporate those portions of the "child-centered pedagogy" which stress knowledge through self-discovery and the incitement of interest in one's own learning, but would also stress the overall context of group learning. Not only can students best learn the practices of democratic discussion, deliberation, and conflict in a collective classroom context, but they also learn the affective lessons of participatory-republican community through group education. Benjamin Rush argued that a method which brings diverse students together to learn common lessons is necessary to republican life, since "young men who have trodden the paths of science together, or have joined in the same sports, whether of swimming, skating, fishing, or hunting, generally feel, through life, such ties to each other as add greatly to the obligations of mutual benevolence."[38] In his discussion of Polish political education, Rousseau was adamant that students be taught together in order to develop public ties, purposes, and affections. This method of collective instruction and interaction among students even extended to recreation, where Rousseau called for the institution of "public games" as a part of the overall education of future Polish citizens:

> The children should not be permitted to play separately according to their fancy, but encouraged to play all together in public; and the games should be conducted in such a way that there is always some common end to which all aspire, to accustom them to common action and to stir up emulation. . . . The important thing is to get them accustomed, from an early age, to rules, to equality, to fraternity, to living under the eyes of their fellow citizens and seeking public approbation.[39]

As with the previous section on the curriculum of citizen education, this discussion of educational method is not meant to be copied directly into a program for classroom instruction, but to illustrate the impact of methods of instruction on citizen education. The way in which the subject matter of civic education is taught has a definite effect on what future citizens learn about democratic politics. A ten-country study of civic education in 1975 showed that instructional method was a critical factor in fostering students who are more knowledgeable, more participant in attitude, and more supportive of democratic values. A classroom climate encouraging discussion among students and active student participation was found to be correlated positively with measures of greater student knowledge, more participant attitudes, and greater support of democratic values, while students in classrooms with more traditional methods of instruction (lecture, rote memorization, little encouragement of student discussion and participation) were found to know less about "civics," and were less participant and less supportive of democratic values (especially of the need for criticism and contention in demo-cratic politics).[40] Educators must realize that the use of classroom methods antithetical to teaching democratic skills and values may counterbalance any gains made through curricular innovation and reform. In thinking about citizen education, we must remember John Dewey's words: "method is not antithetical to subject matter; it is the effective direction of subject matter to desired results."[41]

NOTES

1. *Coming of Age in America* (New York: Random House, 1963), 40.

2. See Samuel Bowles and Herbert Gintis, *Schooling in Capitalist America* (New York: Basic Books, 1972), 36–39; Silberman, *Crisis in the Classroom*, 60, 124; Mary Metz, *Classroom and Corridors: The Crisis of Authority in Desegregated Secondary Schools* (University of California Press, 1978), especially 243.

3. Elizabeth Bennett, "An Ounce of Prevention," in *Discipline in the Classroom* (Washington: National Education Association, 1969).

4. Ronald Gross and Paul Osterman, eds., *High School* (New York: Simon and Schuster, 1971), 14.

5. Silberman, *Crisis in the Classroom*, 134–35.

6. Merelman, "Democratic Politics," 320.

7. Ibid., 325.

8. Joseph D'Amico, "Reviving Student Participation," *Educational Leadership* (October 1980), 45. See also Ralph Tyler, "The Total Educational Environment," in *Education for Responsible Citizenship*, 15–26; Dan Conrad and Diane Hedin, "Citizenship Education Through Participation," in Ibid., 133–154; Paul Beck and M. Kent Jennings, "Pathways to Participation," *American Political Science Review* 76, no. 1 (1982): 94–108.

9. Quoted in Passow, *Secondary Education Reform*, 41. See also *The Adolescent, Other Citizens, and Their High Schools* (New York: McGraw-Hill Book Company, 1975), chap. 9.

10. Gross and Osterman, eds., *High School*, 209–10.

11. See Conrad and Hedin, "Citizenship Education Through Participation." Both the Carnegie Foundation's report cited above and the Coleman Report (Panel on Youth of the President's Science Advisory Committee, *Youth: Transition to Adulthood* [Chicago: University of Chicago Press, 1974]) called for community participation as a means of bridging the gap between generations and between community and students.

12. Alexis de Tocqueville, *Democracy in America* (New York: Vintage Books, 1945), vol. 2, bk. 2: 115.

13. Ibid., 115.

14. Ibid., 117.

15. Ibid., 127.

16. Ibid., 125.

17. Locke, *Of the Conduct*, 73.

18. Rousseau, *Emile*, 205.

19. *The Reform of Secondary Education*, 74.

20. Margaret Mead, "Thinking Ahead: Why Is Education Obsolete?," *Harvard Business Review* (November/December 1958).

21. Dewey, *Democracy and Education*, 158–59.

22. Paolo Friere, *The Pedagogy of the Oppressed* (New York: Continuum Publishing Corp., 1970).

23. Mead, "Thinking Ahead."

24. Dewey, *Democracy and Education*, 158.

25. Antonio Gramsci, in *From Antonio Gramsci: Selections From Political Writings, 1910–1920*, ed. Quintin Hoare (New York: International Publishers, 1971), 11.

26. Of course, the "social sciences disciplines" approach to the civics curriculum is a revival of sorts of a subject-centered method of instruction.

27. Harvard Graduate School of Education Center for Field Studies, *Watertown: The Education of Its Children* (1967), quoted in Silberman, *Crisis in the Classroom*, 150.

28. Dewey, *Democracy and Education*, 305.

29. John Dewey, *The Child and The Curriculum* (Chicago: University of Chicago Press, 1915), 29.

30. Cremin, *Transformation of the School*, 103. See his discussion of American Freudians and their influence on child-centered pedagogy, 211ff.

31. Peter Marin, "The Open Truth and the Fiery Vehemence of Youth," in Gross and Osterman, eds., *High School*, 44.

32. *The Reform of Secondary Education*, p. 99. The report concludes that "the student's personal characteristics and tastes must determine the school or the program in which he enrolls" (102).

33. See Marshall McLuhan and George Leonard, "Learning in the Global Village," in Richard Gross and Ronald Gross, eds., *Radical School Reform* (New York: Simon and Schuster, 1969), 106–15.

34. Mill, *Logic*, 921–922. See chap. 2, 31–33. However, other liberals, like Ackerman, see a completely child-centered curriculum as the proper educational companion to the liberal notion of the self and politics; see Ackerman, *Social Justice in the Liberal State* (Yale University Press, 1980), 156–157.

35. Gramsci, "On Education " 31.

36. Dewey, *Democracy and Education*, 39.

37. Phillip Jackson, "Comprehending a Well-Run Comprehensive," 91.

38. Rush, "Thoughts Upon the Mode of Education," 10. Dewey argues that one can learn things individually but that one only learns their *meaning* in "a context of work and play in association with others," *Democracy and Education*, 358–59. A contemporary argument for group learning methods can be found in Elizabeth Cagan, "Individualism, Collectivism, and Radical Education Reform," *Harvard Education Review* (1978), pp. 47–50.

39. Rousseau, *The Government of Poland*, 21–22.

40. Torney, et al., *Civic Education in Ten Countries*, 327–35.

41. Dewey, *Democracy and Education*, 165.

CHAPTER 6

School Structure
and Citizen Education

W E HAVE JUST EXAMINED the role of the curriculum, of texts, and of methods of instruction on the education of democratic citizens in American secondary schools. But many contemporary writers argue that the current crisis in educational institutions is so severe that it is not enough to fiddle with the curriculum, to change texts and our approach to them, or to make reforms in methods of classroom instruction. For these educational reformers, the system of public schools as it is presently instituted is the greatest barrier to proper learning. Only when the very structure of public schooling in America is changed, they say, will children truly begin to become educated. We must now explore a few of the proposed reforms of educational structures and their possible effect on citizenship education. We will look in particular at the "back-to-basics" movement, the "open schooling" approach, systems of education vouchers, and proposals for "deschooling" American society. We should note that there is a strong relationship between proposed structural reforms of educational institutions and our prior discussion of methods, in that any structural changes would change the method of classroom instruction; but structural reforms go beyond discussions of method in that they involve the basic configuration of the schools themselves.

"Back-to-Basics"

The "back-to-basics" movement views the crisis in citizenship education and in education in general as the result of decades of progressive education, in which fundamental skills and values have been overlooked in order to teach "experience," "life-adjustment," "social problems," and "the new math." The corresponding lack of school discipline, they believe, has been responsible for a deterioration in order and respect among students. Highly publicized declines in students' achievement test scores and in survey measures of knowledge about civics, government, and the Constitution have led many people in the last decade to call for a restructuring of the schools to provide for a more "basic" education.

Proponents of basic education (also called "fundamental" or "traditional" education) call for the establishment of schools in which the basic skills of reading, writing, speaking, spelling, and computation (as opposed to more conceptual topics in mathematics) are taught to students of all grades. This would be combined in secondary schools with instruction in basic science, higher mathematics (still primarily computational), and American history and heritage. Basic schooling at all levels would include the instilling of patriotism and values of individual moral character in students. To address the problem of discipline which many see as critical, "basics" schools are to operate in an atmosphere of order and hierarchical control designed "to reinforce parental teaching of citizenship, respect, discipline, and personal responsibility."[1] An administrator of a fundamental high school in Kentucky described it as "a place dedicated to the highest competence in fundamental skills, patriotism, courtesy, respect, responsibility and citizenship."[2]

Citizenship education in fundamental schools is conceived of exclusively as instilling a sense of unquestioning patriotism and loyalty to one's country. George Weber, associate director of the Council for Basic Education, puts it this way:

> There is a need for a kind of civic education which gives young children, particularly, the idea that their country is a pretty good place. I think we have gone much too far in many schools in concentrating on the deficiencies and warts in American history and American life—so that children and young people get the idea that maybe America is an

awful place to live, and they'd be much better off in communist China.[3]

In their approach to civic education, back-to-basics schools stress saluting the flag, reciting pledges of allegiance, singing patriotic songs, and memorizing fundamental principles and lessons of American government.

Of course, there is also the implicit civic education that comes from the very structure and atmosphere of fundamental schools. Students are drilled in basic lessons of mathematical computation and grammar, writing, and spelling. They are asked in history and civics classes to "memorize and recite parts of speeches and poems that stress American ideals."[4] And they are asked constantly to compete in strictly graded tests of "basic achievement" and "minimum competency." Add to this the overall school atmosphere of stringent discipline (through dress and behavior codes and the constant monitoring of student activity in and out of class), and students get lessons in passive obedience to persons in positions of authority, less emphasis on critical thinking, competition rather than fellowship with their classmates, and the values of conformity and conventional behavior.

On one level, the back-to-basics movement has some merit. Educators have tended to neglect basic skills and values over the past years, and for whatever reason, it is well-documented that students today are graduating from high school with less knowledge of the basics than students of previous years. In fact, many graduate as functional illiterates. A degree of minimum competency in basic subject areas would seem a valid requirement for all citizens, especially given the knowledge required to decide on today's complex political issues. In this sense, back-to-basics proponents are correct in attacking the incompetent education which goes on in many of our high schools.

For the most part, however, the educational changes proposed by advocates of fundamental schools are not at all conducive to the education of democratic citizens. First of all, the narrow conception of learning which underlies the back-to-basics movement fails to encompass the breadth and depth of knowledge necessary to citizens in a democracy. Certainly a foundation in "basic skills" is necessary to any further learning and living, but to limit education in schools to mere rote memorization and drilling in basic skills and subjects is to limit the citizen's capacity to deal with the broad range of complex issues that come up in the course of her or his public life. Dewey argued against the educational fundamentalists of his day, feeling that a course of study featuring just the "basics" was not "broadly human" enough for citizens in a democratic society:

> The notion that the "essentials" of education are the three R's me-chanically treated, is based upon the ignorance of the essentials needed for the realization of democratic ideals. [A curriculum based on] mechanical efficiency in reading, writing, spelling, and figuring, together with the attainment of a certain amount of muscular dexterity . . . implies a somewhat parasitic cultivation bought at the expense of not having the enlightenment and discipline which come from concern with the deepest problems of common humanity. A curriculum which acknowledges the social responsibility of education must present situa-tions where problems are relevant to the problems of living together, and where observation and information are calculated to develop so-cial insight and interest.[5]

If, as political theorists concerned with education were seen to suggest above, a curriculum which integrates a wide range of intel-lectual subject matter is most appropriate to developing democratic citizenship attributes, then proponents of back-to-basics in educa-tion too narrowly circumscribe the curriculum in their schools.

It is not just the back-to-basics *curriculum* that is ill-conceived, however. The very method of instruction and the entire atmosphere permeating basic schools is also detrimental to citizenship educa-tion. First of all, going back to an earlier discussion, a "basic" ap-proach to reading is aimed at developing literal, mechanical readers, rather than the kind of critical readers and thinkers re-quired in a democracy. Further, the rigorous discipline and the stress against contention and critical thinking in fundamental schools may not allow for the development of people who can air and resolve differences and conflicts in the public realm. This kind of atmosphere, contrary to its proponents' beliefs, does not create the kinds of deep-seated democratic values and attitudes that come from controversial discussion and participation in debates over democratic ideals and policies. In addition, though basic education professes a commitment to patriotism, it does not pay attention to the creation of bonds to local political communities and smaller associations (rather than "the nation"), nor does it foster participation as the source of a citizen's development of affective ties to the polity. Hence, even the patriotism and love of country that educational fundamentalists stress is hollow, lacking both the deep-seated cognitive foundation and the active participation in a community of fellow citizens (or future citizens) which undergirds democratic patriotism under the participatory-republican conception.

The back-to-basics movement may force educators to focus more attention on improving student knowledge of basic skills and values, and for this it is to be applauded. Democratic citizens need to possess the kinds of basic skills and knowledge which will allow them to be productive members of society and to participate in making political decisions. But the back-to-basics proposals go no deeper than this in really solving the crisis of democratic citizenship we are currently experiencing. To improve civic education in America we must look to other structural alternatives.

"Open Schools"

On the flip side of the educational reformist coin from the proponents of basic education lies the movement for "open schools." Proponents of open schooling feel that the schools as presently constituted stifle student creativity and self-esteem and prevent learning from taking place.

Open schooling takes the spirit of the child-centered approach and applies it across the board in restructuring the school environment. Open schools are founded upon the belief, expressed by Roland Barth, that "children have both the competence and the right to make significant decisions concerning their own learning,"[6] and the entire educational atmosphere reflects that belief. In open schools, the structured classroom is abolished, with "interest areas" or "nooks" replacing rows of desks and chairs, and large time blocks replacing the traditional class period (based on the contention articulated by George Leonard that "if human beings are individual and unique, then any system of fixed scheduling and mass instruction must be insanely inefficient"[7]). Most of the "coercive" aspects of conventional schools, such as grades, exams, or a set curriculum, are also either abolished or relaxed under an open school system, to allow for the emergence of "unfettered genius" and "creativity" in students.

Open schools also transform the role of the teacher, making him or her at most a *facilitator* of the individual child's *direct* learning experience:

> The teacher's place in this model is somewhere *outside* the learning process. The teacher's role is to provide the conditions which will make the child's active exploration of the real world both likely and fruitful. Thus, there is a mutual interchange between the child, the world, and the teacher, but it is *the child* who is the principal agent of his *own* learning.[8]

The teacher is seen by "open educators" as a mere "enabler," an "adult in the classroom" who acts as an inactive "lubricant" in the child's learning process. The overall atmosphere in an open school is best characterized by George Leonard: "While the children are on the school grounds, they are *absolutely* free to go and do *anything* they wish that does not hurt someone else. They are *free learners.*"[9]

Like basic education, open education fails to provide an alternative structure for citizenship education, on a number of grounds. First, open schools tend merely to remove those aspects of the traditional school structure which restrain individuals in their quest for learning, without creating new structures or arrangements to take their place. Released from the traditional curriculum and its strictures, open schools often turn classes into "extended rap sessions" or unstructured environments where students can move at will and do whatever they please. And with the teacher removed from an active position in the learning process, little remains to give meaning or structure to the individual student's unsullied "learning experiences." In conceiving of themselves in this way, open schools forget that for the adolescent, education is a continuing process of identifying with and differentiating him- or herself from his or her culture, community, and surroundings, and their values and ideals. As such, education involves the confrontation of a student with the self and other students, with a discipline or body of knowledge, and with the teacher. The argument of most proponents of open education, that a grab bag of courses or experiences initiated by the student's own immediate interests is an adequate substitute for a coherently structured curriculum, denies adolescents both the cognitive learning experience of grappling with their culture and history, and the affective experience necessary for them to care for their community while also situating themselves within and against it. Only by coming into contact with the community's life and history in some kind of structured manner can individuals make the choices and decisions necessary to becoming full persons *and* citizens, able to carry on the community's projects and purposes into the future.[10]

Furthermore, open schooling suffers from some of the same social misconceptions as does a completely child-centered curriculum. With its emphasis on establishing the individual as the sole authority in her or his own education, the open school movement often neglects important *civic learning* experiences that can be obtained only in a collective classroom setting. Like the method of individualized instruction, open education seems obsessed with the self and its isolated experiences, failing to realize that "democracy involves both authority and an intrinsically social consciousness on the part of individuals."[11]

The direct effect of open schools on civic education is unambiguous. Being primarily interested in the structure of elementary schools, proponents of "open" or "free" schools rarely concern themselves with citizenship education as such, but most such educators show contempt for the traditional civics curriculum of history and government due to what they see as their "irrelevance" to students.[12] When the citizenship education goals of open education *are* discussed, they are usually articulated as the development of "critical thinking," without any foundation for such criticism. In the case of the "new kind of citizenship education" to be taught in George Leonard's free schools, its conception is completely vacuous, involving the goal of learning "heightened awareness and control of emotional, sensory, and bodily states, and through this, increased empathy for other people."[13] Open education as an answer to current school structure is as inappropriate to the education of democratic citizens as a back-to-basics approach.

Education Vouchers

Because they cannot transform all existing schools, some proponents of both basic schools and open schools have called for some type of educational voucher or subsidy system. Under such a system, parents would be given publicly funded tuition certificates which they could then use to send their child to any school, public or private, which participates in the voucher system. Although not a specific program of structural school reform, a voucher system would have great ramifications on the structure of secondary schooling in America. And given the increased public acceptance it has been receiving over the past few years, the implications of an educational voucher system for the education of democratic citizens are important to discuss.

Milton Friedman was one of the earliest advocates of a voucher system in education.[14] Friedman proposed establishing a system containing both public and private schools, where parents would be paid "a sum equal to the estimated cost of educating a child in a public school," if they sent their child to an "approved" private school. These private schools would be able to set their own curriculum and admissions policies, and would operate like producers in the marketplace, trying to attract parents to consume their product. Friedman's reasoning was that a voucher system would most effectively represent all parents and students, and make educators finally accountable in the marketplace. Friedman argued that the competition which would ensue from this free market approach would stimulate the "development and improvement of all schools." Parents would no longer be coerced into sending children to ineffective public schools (or else asked to "pay twice" for education if they sent them to private schools), and governments would no longer regulate mediocrity in schools and in teachers through their rigid and ineffective requirements about building or classroom size or teacher certification.

In more recent years, versions of Friedman's plan have been endorsed by other educational thinkers. Most prominent among them is James Coleman, whose most recent study comparing student achievement in private and public schools showed that private school students did better on cognitive achievement tests than students from public schools, controlling for other variables. His study also showed that, contrary to what opponents of private schools contend, only in the area of religious segregation was there a significant demographic difference between private and public schools on the whole—there was no overall difference between private and public schools on measures of racial segregation, and private schools were only slightly higher on measures of the economic segregation of students. Coleman concludes from this study that it is in the public interest to provide some form of tuition credit system for parents choosing to send children to private schools:

> The public interest in common institutions is not an *overriding* public interest. It is a relatively weak public interest when measured against the public interest in helping all children, particularly those of the disadvantaged, receive a better education. It is a relatively weak public interest when measured against the interests of children who are being directly and manifestly harmed by the school environment in which they find themselves, but who are unable to escape that environment.[15]

The most recent voucher proposal engendering national attention and debate was one which appeared as an initiative on the California ballot in November 1982. Called "An Initiative for Education by Choice," it was authored by John Coons and Stephen Sugarman, and proposed creating two new types of schools in addition to public schools: Independent Public Schools and Family Choice Schools (the difference between them being that in the latter religion could be taught). Parents sending children to these participating alternative schools would receive publicly financed vouchers for 90 percent of what it costs to send a child to the regular public schools. Unlike the Friedman proposal, however, the Initiative for Education by Choice would set statewide basic requirements which must be met by all participating schools—requirements about each school's public dissemination of information about itself, about the extent to which religious belief can be taught in schools, and, most important, about mandated low-income admissions in all participating schools (set at 25 percent of student capacity). The Coons-Sugarman initiative was an attempt to combine the desirability of parents' free choice when it comes to their children's schooling, which characterizes other voucher proposals, with strict regulations mandating low-income student admissions in all schools, which reflects a legitimate concern about the uses of voucher systems to achieve racial or economic segregation.[16]

Arguments in favor of educational voucher systems are couched primarily in terms of the individual's right to receive a high-quality education that meets his or her needs and interests. Voucher proponents say that they would provide parents from all social and economic backgrounds with the freedom to choose from a variety of schools the one that would best meet their children's needs and educational interests. One of Coons's major arguments is that the public school system today is a voucher system for the rich (who can move to wealthy neighborhoods and thereby attend good schools) and means compulsory poor quality schooling for the poor.[17] To the extent that a voucher system would open up opportunities to all children to get an "individualized" education that would meet their particular curricular and methodological interests, this would no longer be true.

Proponents argue that the use of education vouchers would also have positive political effects. To the extent that a voucher system would encourage parents actively to seek out information about different schools and their offerings and then choose among them, it would bring about greater participation among people in the positive act of choosing their children's education. Coons contends that families who participate in choosing their schools are more likely to be active participants in the schools' life and governance and more public-minded, at least as regards the "community" of their children's schools. Citizens would be taking over authority in educational decision-making that had been previously held in the hands of state and school bureaucrats. Voucher systems could even mandate policy boards for each school, consisting of parents, teachers, administrators, and even students, thereby increasing democratic control over education and providing "civic lessons" for those participants in the running of their local schools.[18]

Moreover, advocates of an educational voucher system maintain that to the extent that the public school today has become increasingly an institution without common purposes, goals, or values—

where many children who do not want to be there are forced to attend, where problems of discipline and bureaucratic mediocrity have caused students to perform more poorly in many measurable cognitive achievement areas, and where children with parents who can afford it have opted out, making the system an increasingly segregated rather than an integrating institution—a voucher system would provide for schools that reflect public purposes. A voucher system could produce a variety of schools with their own "publics," and could rejuvenate the public schools to provide clientele services in the face of competition, bringing about a number of decentralized, face-to-face communities of common interest and purpose. In fact, some thinkers, though they may lament the decay of public schools, think that increasingly it is only private schools that can create the "communities of value" so important to public (and citizen) education. Increasingly, they say, only private schools may "have a public in the classical sense."[19]

Of course, many of these arguments assume the most ideal conditions for an educational voucher system. None of the proposals have so far *mandated* decision-making policy boards consisting of all parties in the private schools participating in the voucher system, and there is strong evidence that many schools (especially sectarian schools) would object to community decision-making concerning school policy. In addition, in an ethnically and religiously diverse society such as ours, a voucher system is likely to create schools divided along lines of homogeneity, further segregating educational experience in America. R. Freeman Butts has argued that a voucher system would probably *not* provide the "overall sense of political community needed for a visible public life."[20]

A major argument against voucher systems, then, is that they would further accelerate the trend toward privatism and away from support for public institutions. Parents would be able to withdraw from yet another public institution, sending their children to separate, specialized schools which could best serve their particular needs and interests. Rather than building common commitments to public purposes and to a potential political community (beginning in the public school), which was one reason public education was first instituted, voucher systems would encourage the pursuit of private interests and desires at the expense of public goals. While vouchers do offer the possibility of creating an active "public" around each individual school, as mentioned before, very little of the voucher movement expresses any concern with maintaining or creating a sense of civic feeling, but instead argues for their case in terms of cultural pluralism and the right to individually meaningful learning. Most parents want to create a climate where their children can perform better on the accepted measures of cognitive achievement and so get ahead in life; they see this as more important than learning the lessons of democratic citizenship. In this sense, voucher systems tend to reflect the liberal conception of education, expressing little concern with creating political commitments or participatory attitudes through public schooling.

Educational voucher systems would have a disastrous effect on citizen education. Since participating schools would probably have very few requirements imposed upon them to create certain programs for civic education, students would be denied both the infusion of a common history and culture through a common program of instruction (important for creating a sense of common heritage and purpose, crucial to the participatory-republican conception) and the skills necessary to be self-governing and fully participating citizens. Without some kind of mandated civics curriculum, the polity cannot ensure that students will have the proper preparation for democratic political life, thus exacerbating the crisis of inadequate citizen education discussed at the outset of this book. Moreover, the very notion of democratic community as a place where people of diverse backgrounds and interests come together out of geographic or other *necessity* to search for common ground and meaning would be dashed by a system of separate schools most likely serving separate, homogeneous groups who do not have to come together at all. It is the necessary character of political association which distinguishes it from other forms of association, which are, to a greater extent, voluntary—and this very distinctiveness is lost under a system of voluntary educational association.

A related problem with voucher systems is that they may increase citizen passivity as well as privatism. While many voucher proponents do contend that vouchers would increase parental involvement in the schools and in educational policy, there is no evidence that this would happen. As mentioned before, most parents are drawn to voucher systems not by the promise of participation in educational policy and thus a renewal of civic life, but rather by the prospect of finding an acceptable school for their children. These parents want to find the kind of school to which they can send their child and not have to act any further, knowing their children's education "is now taken care of." In fact, a voucher system would encourage parents to think that they have done enough in sending their child to an alternative school which embodies their educational philosophy—thus the choice of school for their child could be their last active political decision, rather than one in a series of such decisions. Everything else would be left up to the school, even more than is now the case with public schools.

Thus, if voucher systems are proposed to provide for better parental control over and participation in their children's schools, it can be easily argued that parental control is likely to be more effective in the long run when undertaken in the public arena, within localized political institutions, rather than in a private contract or bargaining agreement with private school owners. In addition, in the public school setting parental actions in the interest of their children will take on a broader political meaning—their actions for their children may improve the whole district for all the community's children. The proposal to replace the public school system—which has the potential, if strengthened and renewed, of providing decentralized community control over education—with a market system which may be unresponsive to public need, does not seem to be the best way of regaining parental (or student) control over schooling.[21]

"Deschooling"

One final alternative which merits consideration is "deschooling." Proponents of "deschooling," most notable among them Ivan Illich[22] and Everett Reimer,[23] argue that other proposed structural reforms, including open schooling and voucher systems, presume the "schooled society" as their foundation and simply build upon the current structure of institutionalized schools. Advocates of "deschooling" see any form of institutionalized schools as creating "monopolies" on learning which lock people into prescribed behavior, a prescribed curriculum of "social control," and, through the demands of school certification, into "conforming cogs" of modern techno-cratic-industrial society. All schools, these thinkers say, teach de-pendence upon others (teachers) for learning, thus encumbering the "free decision making" of "free people . . . choosing freely as indi-viduals" among an array of educational alternatives and *direct* learn-ing experiences.[24] Illich declares that though teaching "may contrib-ute to certain kinds of learning under certain circumstances . . . most people acquire most of their knowledge outside school, and in school only insofar as school, in a few rich countries, has become their place of confinement during an increasing part of their lives."[25] Instead of equalizing everybody's chances for learning and growth, the promotion of "universal education," according to Illich, has merely allowed the school system to monopolize the distribution and type of educational chances, thus pacifying and controlling stu-dents rather than liberating them through intellectual growth.[26] Our reliance on schools as institutions, he says, has brought about "psy-chological impotence" and "spiritual helplessness" in a people sup-posed to be self-reliant and self-governing. Illich concludes that "by making men abdicate the responsibility for their own growth, schools lead many to a kind of spiritual suicide."[27]

As an alternative to the present school structure, deschooling advocates like Illich offer an educational plan consisting of "four networks of learning." First, Illich calls for the opening up of direct access to "educational tools" or "instruments" for the learner. Stu-dents would be given complete access to machines, natural pre-serves, games, and other things in the world around them, to learn from them directly as they saw fit: "The general physical environ-ment must be made accessible, and those physical learning re-sources which have been reduced to teaching instruments must become generally available for self-directed learning."[28]

For "fundamental skills" such as languages or mathematics, Illich would provide "skill centers" where those who possessed these skills could provide uninstitutionalized "drill instruction" to those re-questing training. The third "network of learning" would be pro-vided by computerized "peer-matching" services. Those who wish to exchange thoughts, ideas, or knowledge on any given subject would be put in touch with one another through a "communications network" established by deschooling advocates, in order to pursue mutual learning experiences outside of any structured setting. These "peer-matching networks" are at the heart of the deschooling educational plan, since they would provide a direct educational experience for students on the basis of equality and free exchange.

Finally, for students desiring "learning experiences" which these three networks could not provide, the deschooler's plan would allow learners to entrust themselves to "intellectual leaders" whom they would choose themselves and whose authority would be based on knowledge and a willingness to share it, rather than an "institutionalized credential."[29] The entire deschooling program is based upon the notion that the learning experience must be taken out of its institutionalized framework in the schools, to be made the product of the individual's independent judgment of his or her own individual needs and interests. For its advocates, deschooling merely means taking the logic of ideas such as "child-centered psychology" and "liberal education" to their ultimate conclusion, thereby making good on the promise of other educators.

There is a sense in which deschooling reflects that part of republican thought which concerns itself with salvaging individual men and women in the face of corrupt (and corrupting) public institutions. The advocates of deschooling *do* feel that schools as institutions have decayed, and have failed to truly educate people. Deschoolers like Illich feel that only by withdrawing from these corrupt public institutions and establishing a more direct and informal educational environment will "the true education of free men, capable of mastering technology rather than being enslaved by it, or by others in its name,"[30] take place. In this light, the attempt to "deschool society" parallels the educational project explicated by Rousseau in *Emile*.

For the most part, however, deschooling reflects an extreme version of the liberal conception of education. Advocates of deschooling want to free the individual learner completely from the strictures of schools or other public institutions. Detached from the schools and their repressive rules and relationships, individual learners, they hold, will be able to exchange intellectual skills in the free marketplace of knowledge. Here deschooling reflects liberal empiricism, which sees knowledge as the outcome of the individual's direct contact with and perception of the environment around him or her. Illich's goal is to "provide the learner with new links to the world instead of continuing to funnel all educational programs through the teacher."[31] This idea conflicts with the participatory-republican psychology of education, which holds that our knowledge of things in the world (as well as ourselves) depends on the conscious mediation between and communication with other people. Participatory-republicans see that we are dependent upon others for our learning, especially our civic learning. Deschooling, though it has much in common with the republican tradition of dealing with corrupt public institutions, is ultimately quite liberal in its major thrust.[32]

Whatever its conceptual origins, deschooling fails to address the problem of civic education. Much like those of open school proponents, Illich's solutions are completely *apolitical* in their emphasis. Solely concerning itself with liberating individuals to provide for their own particular educational needs, deschooling does not consider the citizenship needs of providing a common historical, cultural, or moral context within which divergent individuals thrown together by necessity can begin to decide on issues of public interest. Deschooling offers none of the political lessons of participation in and commitment to common goals or ideals, and none of the political knowledge and skills essential to citizens in a democracy. Deschooling's ideal type is the individual, detached from any ties to those around him or her, unfettered by school requirements of compulsory attendance or minimum curricular standards, able to make free exchanges and contracts for his or her own perceived educational needs. Illich's vision, then, is not of the student as citizen, but as entrepreneur. Illich even admits that the political order itself is endangered by any attempts at deschooling. But since he believes that learning and living are "personal activities" whose ends cannot be to serve "the state" or any other extrinsic political entity, he also believes that this kind of danger to the polity is a good thing.[33]

Rather than look to any of the major structural reforms just discussed, all of which have major problems in terms of democratic citizenship education, we might instead attempt to focus on strengthening the educational institutions which already exist in

America. Most of the reforms proposed, such as open schools, voucher systems, or deschooling, call for new educational structures which would encourage more individualized education. In light of the failures of the present public school system, these reforms offer educational options more responsive to particular individual needs in learning (in this, back-to-basics education is also responding to a particular clientele, proposing a structure whichs meets certain student certification and achievement interests). But if we take even a part of the participatory-republican conception of education seriously, it is clear that both the skills necessary to democratic deliberation and decision-making and the affective bonds essential to democratic community are best developed by an educational structure and method in which learning takes place collectively, in the common classroom.

The comprehensive public high school, a uniquely American contribution to educational systems, may provide the best structure for the participatory-republican conception of politics and citizen education. Ideally, the comprehensive high school brings together a heterogeneous population of students, with different backgrounds, interests, and professional and vocational ambitions, to instruct them in common lessons and values. In terms of size and format, the comprehensive high school meets the face-to-face requirements of participatory-republican politics, since most schools have between 400 and 4000 students, divided into small classes. With a proper curriculum and methods, the high school classroom can thus be turned into an embryonic community association, with students engaging each other (and the teacher) in lively discussion and deliberation over political matters. In terms of curriculum, the comprehensive public high school can better expose students to a diversity of disciplines under the same roof. And in terms of governance, the comprehensive high school can be readily brought under the democratic control of the entire community in and around the school itself.

If the object of citizen education is to prepare the young to enter into and cope with the life of the political community, the comprehensive high school ideally represents a perfect mediating institution between the family and the polity.[34] As James Conant argues, the comprehensive public high school "endeavors to provide a general education for all future citizens on the basis of a common democratic understanding,"[35] and may therefore be the proper instrument of a democratic citizenship education. Proponents of alternative educational structures assume that the choice is between the public schools in their current disarray and their own idealized conceptions of a proper school system. In fact, the choice may really be between their proposals, which are likely to create the kinds of serious problems for the education of citizens discussed earlier in this chapter, and a commitment to renew and reform the public high schools. If this is true, the latter course is the best possible guarantee of structures conducive to democratic citizen education. Possibilities for revitalizing the comprehensive public high school will be discussed in the conclusion.

NOTES

1. James K. Wellington, "American Education: Its Failure and Its Future," *Phi Delta Kappan* 58, no. 7 (March 1977): 527–30; George Weber, "Looking at Back to Basics," Eric Clearinghouse for Social Sciences Education, *Annual Newsletter* (Washington: ERIC, November 1976); Richard Vetterli, *Storming the Citadel: The Fundamental Revolution Against Progressive Education* (Costa Mesa, California: Educational Media Press, 1976); Burton Yales Pines, *Back to Basics* (New York: William Morrow and Co., 1982), chap. 4.

2. Jean S. Ruffra, "Back to Basics" (Washington: ERIC, 1977).

3. Weber, "Looking at Back to Basics."

4. Ruffra, "Back to Basics."

5. Dewey, *Democracy and Education*, 192.

6. Roland Barth, *Open Education and the American School* (New York: Agathon Press, 1972), 56.

7. George Leonard, *Education and Ecstasy* (New York: Delacorte Press, 1968), 181.

8. Barth, *Open Education*, 60–62.

9. Leonard, *Education and Ecstasy*, 141.

10. See Erik Erikson, "Youth: Fidelity and Diversity," *Daedalus* (Winter 1962). See also Silberman, *Crisis in the Classroom*, 334–36; Donald Oliver, *Education and Community* (Berkeley: McCutchan Publishing Corp., 1976), 40–43.

11. Bowles and Gintis, *Schooling in Capitalist America*, 252. However, the "revolutionary" educational guidelines which Bowles and Gintis propose conceive of democracy as solely economic democracy, not concerning themselves with political citizenship outside of the workplace; see pp. 287–288.

12. For a good example of this, see Leonard's discussion of Thucydides in *Education and Ecstasy*, 171–74.

13. Ibid., 132.

14. Milton Friedman, *Capitalism and Freedom* (Chicago: University of Chicago Press, 1962), 85–107.

15. Coleman, "Private Schools, Public Schools, and the Public Interest," *Public Interest* (Summer 1981): 29–30; see also Coleman, *High School and Beyond: A Longitudinal Study for the 1980s, Public and Private Schools* (Chicago: National Opinion Research Council, 1981), for the study results.

16. The arguments for this type of voucher system are found in John Coons and Steven Sugarman, *Education by Choice: The Case For Family Control* (Berkeley: University of California Press, 1978), and more recently defended in Coons, "Reply to R. Freeman Butts," *Phi Delta Kappan* (September 1979): 10–13.

17. Coons, "Reply to Butts," 10–11. See also Christopher Jencks and Judith Areen, "Education Vouchers: A Proposal for Diversity and Choice," *Teachers College Record* (February 1971).

18. In fact, Coons and Sugarman recognize that a voucher system without such policy boards would probably be counter to the whole idea of a voucher system as a system of free choice.

19. Gerald Grant, "The Character of Education and the Education of Character," *Daedalus* (Summer 1981): 135–148.

20. R. Freeman Butts, "Educational Vouchers: The Public Pursuit of the Private Purse," *Phi Delta Kappan* (September 1979): 7–9.

21. This is also argued by Michael Walzer in *Radical Principles* (New York: Basic Books, Inc., 1980), chap. 8. A possible alternative is offered by educational writer Mario Fantini. He has proposed that instead of a voucher system consisting of participating private and public schools, we institute an "internal voucher system" in the public sector. The polity would establish different types of schools to serve students with different interests, but within the public school system, all under the control of the local community. Still, students within the schools in this system would be segregated according to specific method of instruction or interests; see Mario Fantini, *Alternative Education: A Sourcebook for Parents, Teachers, Students, and Administration* (New York: Anchor Doubleday, 1976), and Fantini, *The People and Their Schools: Community Participation* (Bloomington, Indiana: Phi Delta Kappa Foundation, 1975).

22. Ivan Illich, *Deschooling Society* (New York: Harper and Row, 1972).

23. Everett Reimer, *School Is Dead: Alternatives in Education* (Garden City: Doubleday, 1970).

24. Ibid., 51–58.

25. Illich, *Deschooling Society*, 18.

26. Ibid., 16–17. See also Stephen Arons, *Compelling Belief: The Culture of American Schooling* (New York: McGraw-Hill, 1983).

27. Ibid., 87.

28. Ibid., 116.

29. Ibid., 20–32.

30. Ibid., 30. See also Reimer, *School is Dead*, 18ff.

31. Illich, *Deschooling Society*, 104.

32. Advocates of "deschooling" seem to reflect a dual conception present in much of American educational thinking, which on the one hand denigrates schools as institutions which enforce conventional standards and a "lowest-common-denominator-culture" suppressing the emergence of "sublime genius" and "intellectual creativity," and on the other hand sees schools as out of touch with the "real world," existing in a sheltered ivory tower that is totally detached from reality outside. This dual critique, which one finds in many proponents of alternative educational arrangements, forgets that democratic citizenship may have to put a damper on public expressions of "unrestrained individual creativity" which can destroy the "polis," and also that *proper* schooling can provide the intellectual and emotional tools by which we *mediate* the real world, neither existing apart from reality or becoming subsumed in it.

33. Illich, *Deschooling Society*, 70–71.

34. See Oliver, *Education and Community*, 8–10; though Oliver sees that the attempt to make schools more communitarian is indeed problematic, given their diversity and the demands placed on them to produce "credentialized professionals."

35. Conant, *The Comprehensive High School*, 4–5.

CHAPTER 7

Cognitive and Affective Citizen Education

MUCH HAS BEEN SAID in the preceding pages about the centrality of an affective component to citizenship education under the participatory-republican conception. According to participatory-republicans, the dual nature of democratic politics, possessed of both cognitive and affective elements, requires civic education to have an affective as well as a cognitive content. The education of democratic citizens should center not only on the individual's intellectual and rational faculties—stressing the use of critical reasoning capacities and the development of sources of cognitive political attitudes—but should also accentuate the building of communal bonds and fraternal feelings of loyalty and responsibility toward fellow citizens. This need for both affective and cognitive components of civic education has important ramifications for current educational practice. But it also may create irreconcilable tensions for individual student-citizens and for the polity attempting to educate them fully. This chapter will consider the justifications for such a dual education, the nature of affective content in the civics curriculum, and the possible tensions created by the combination of affective and cognitive instruction.

In its curricular goals and practices, contemporary American citizenship education tends to concentrate on building cognitive knowledge and skills. Since the report of the famous Committee of Ten in 1893, which said that the chief purpose of education was "to train the mind," the main thrust among American educators has been cognitive development. The task of training vast numbers of professionals and specialists from the turn of the century onward has dictated that students come out of schools with certain bodies of knowledge and a commitment to "clear and sound thinking."[1] All extra-cognitive education (with the exception of physical education, of course—"sound body, sound mind") is considered for the most part superfluous and sometimes even dangerous, given the contemporary belief that attitudes and values ought not be "imposed" upon students in the classroom.

This has been no less true of civics instruction than of mathematics or science. The concern over indoctrination and the inability to reach agreement on values has made even the in-depth study of the sources of *cognitive* belief (democratic ideas and values) disappear from the civics curriculum, let alone any affective lessons of citizenship. If we look at the various approaches to citizen education in recent years, we can see an overriding concern with cognitive lessons to the detriment of affective content. This is certainly true of the "social science disciplines" approach, as its proponents are basically interested in the development of cognitive faculties and bodies of knowledge in students. It is also the case with the moral development and values clarification approaches discussed in chapter 4. Kohlberg and associates are interested strictly in the *cognitive* moral development of students as a means to developing better citizens, not in the affective components of moral development or democratic citizenship. And the advocates of values clarification are interested only in the cognitive process of valuing—they are wary of any infusion of cognitive beliefs as a basis for democratic politics.

The monolithic concern with cognitive education is also characteristic of "critical education," an approach to citizen education especially admired by contemporary "radical" and leftist educators. Advocates of a more "critical" approach to education want above all to teach students to use "critical rationality" which will then move them "to challenge the social, political, and economic forces that weigh so heavily upon their lives." Students, these thinkers say, must be made to question all "canonized" knowledge and values through a program which involves students in (1) participating in producing and criticizing "classroom meanings"; (2) being taught to think critically; (3) appropriating "their own histories"; and (4) learning about the structural and ideological forces which influence and restrict people's lives and structure the values we hold.[2] Since "critical educators" feel that the teaching of values or affective lessons in education are used only to "legitimize class interests," they want to "take schools out of the business of making attitudes."[3]

This concern with developing "critical rationality," then, does not recognize that an affective component might underlie such cognitive dispositions. In this, proponents of "critical education" are mistaken. People who care for their fellow citizens as a part of a political community and for the values and goals that underlie democratic society are much better able to criticize departures from such ideals and act collectively to combat them than their peers who do not care. In fact, without an ethical (common devotion to common values and ideals) or affective (feelings of solidarity with fellow citizens) foundation, advocates of "critical rationality" as the predominant goal of civic education have nothing in which to ground such criticism except self-interest or some set of imposed universal cognitive principles (which they themselves discount as "reflecting class interests"). As Josiah Royce argues, not only does such an education in "critical rationality" leave the *citizen* without attachments or common purposes, but it also leaves the *individual* empty, without the purpose and unity (which Royce feels comes from what he calls "loyalty") to give his or her own life meaning.[4]

We have argued that in their conception of and approach to the overall civics curriculum, contemporary American educators have tended consciously to overlook important affective objectives in their quest for higher levels of cognitive achievement. But the benefits of greater student knowledge may be offset by the diminishing quality of citizen character and behavior that comes from pursuing cognitive goals to the neglect of affective lessons of citizenship. Paul Goodman argues that educators have already lost the ability to imbue deep-seated feelings for community and country in our future citizens: "For the first time in recorded history, the mention of country, community, place has lost its power to animate."[5] Goodman sees this as a "tragic loss," since "community spirit and patriotism is the conviction in which it is possible to grow up.["6] No amount of cognitive knowledge can make up for this lack of affective political feeling.

Though he wrote at the end of the eighteenth century, Samuel Doggett articulated the same concern that agitates all participatory-republicans interested in the civic responsibility of the secondary schools:

> While unwearied pains have been taken to give learning to youth, to give them skill in the arts and knowledge in the sciences, the habitudes of the *heart*, their dispositions, tastes, and sentiments, on which moral character is grafted, have been too much neglected. . . . We have the unhappiness sometimes to see souls widely expanded in knowledge awfully maciated with the dark shades of vice: angels in understanding, devils in conduct.[7]

Compare this statement to a contemporary educator's criticism of the purely cognitive, "skills-oriented" approach to citizenship education now practiced in most American secondary schools:

> Without the ethical basis—the goals and values of citizens— citizenship skills do not begin to constitute citizenship; indeed, without reference to some goal or other they are pointless. . . . *Good citizenship is no more a purely cognitive matter than is morality,* and therefore *it is necessary to give children more than skills and method. They must be made to care, feel, and identify in certain ways.* . . . Those who intellectualize citizenship education to the point of limiting it to skills and competencies can have no hope of creating citizens who care in the ways mentioned (emphasis added).[8]

Under a participatory-republican conception of democratic citizenship, then, the education of the affections is as important to the secondary school student as education in cognitive skills and knowledge. Rousseau articulated one of the more complete justifications for affective content in what we would today call "secondary education." He held that the first sentiment in a young adolescent was friendship ("the first act of his nascent imagination is to teach him that he has fellows"). He saw the adolescent as "drawn by the first movements of nature toward the tender and affectionate passions"; typically, he or she is "moved by the sufferings of his fellows" and "has a thrill of satisfaction at seeing his comrade."[9] Because adolescence is the age of "comiseration, clemency and generosity" (rather than "vengeance and hate"), the task of the educator according to Rousseau is to "form the heart" (or "moderate" it) during these years in ways that will allow the student to participate positively later in public life rather than ultimately shunning and despising it.[10] The teacher must make the student feel that he "is a man like others";[11] he must encourage attachments to and identity with the larger community around him. Only by building in students the affective feelings toward their fellow citizens can the foundation for a democratic political community be established.[12] In fact, as the life of the political community progresses and becomes more complex over time, and as common goals and purposes are needed and sought more often by citizens, the importance of a basic affection between and encouragement among citizens grows.[13] If they are not cultivated in the civic education of the young, the affective bonds necessary to the continued success of democratic politics will not develop.

Following this argument, a proper citizenship education would be one which combines cognitive and affective instruction. Tocqueville believed that support for a democratic republic was strongest "where the instruction which enlightens the understanding is not separated from the moral education which amends the heart."[14] Both the cognitive skills and correlative affective lessons are best taught through some of the curricular devices discussed earlier as reforms to the high school curriculum. A civics curriculum which is broad in scope and content, incorporating the humanities as well as the social and natural sciences, is more likely to encourage the affective (as well as the cognitive) attributes of democratic citizenship than the narrow "government" sequence currently in place in most schools. A method of instruction which is collective and cooperative, rather than individualized and competitive, is most conducive to creating a context in which citizens come together to share experiences and deliberate about common concerns. And a high school program which includes participation both in and out of class as an important component of citizen education will have affective as well as cognitive benefits. Students who participate together in school and community projects will learn not only the skills and knowledge involved in democratic political action, but also to care for their fellow participants.

Students who are taught the affective attributes of loyalty to and love for fellow citizens and for the polity as a whole, as well as the cognitive skills of critical thinking, verbal reasoning, and the ability to engage in political conflict and its transformation, will be the inheritors and preservers of the future of American democracy. They will be able to engage in common projects and participate in debates characterized by contentious discussion among people who are diverse, independent, and knowledgeable about the policies best suited to their interests, and by the mutual feeling that the political community and its members count for enough to work out their conflicts, to arrive at a unified policy or law. The combination of affective and cognitive components is the ideal of the participatory-republican conception of democratic politics, which Royce said brings to its citizens the "cordial solidarity of national spirit [which] if it has discouraged strident self-assertion, it has not suppressed individual judgment."[15]

But there are strong tensions involved in such a "dialectical" citizenship education. The cognitive content of democratic political education may collide inevitably with the affective content of such education. An education stressing critical reasoning and the legitimacy of divergent opinions and interests can have a subversive effect upon any attempt to create and maintain group cohesion, since diversity and conflict on important issues can tear citizens apart. Dealing with a problem of fundamental concern, the rational individual whose cognitive abilities have been educated may not be predisposed to listen to others, or to resolve conflicting interests in the final formulation of public policy. Citizens whose critical thinking and reasoning skills are fully developed might have difficulty obeying the will of the polity when it squarely opposes their own interest or cognitive knowledge about which public course is best. If such citizens perceive the burden of community loyalty to be oppressive at times, this in turn may begin to break down their affective bonds toward the polity. The tension here between the skills and processes necessary to democratic discussion and decision-making (mostly cognitive) and the affective ties that undergird and reinforce such processes seems intrinsic to democratic politics.

On the other hand, the internalizing of affective lessons of citizenship may stunt the proper growth of cognitive concerns. People who learn to love their fellow citizens may then be reticent to engage in strident debates over policy or law, even though their interests and knowledge would incline them to disagree with their neighbors. The very conflict necessary to spur a true democratic political resolution (one based on the airing of all interests and differences and final agreement on a common interest rather than immediate acquiescence to one group's particular interests or perception of the public good) may be blocked by civic affections and solidarity.[16]

Furthermore, part of the affective teaching of citizenship is that some areas of public belief or value are beyond question. Democratic citizens come to feel loyalty to and faith in certain fundamental principles which hold them together as a political community, and which they dare not challenge. There may be a fine line between what should and should not be questioned or criticized, and the democratic ideal of full participation and open discussion to arrive at the best public policy may collide with the community's heartfelt desire to hold fast to certain beliefs. Bertrand Russell recognized the tension involved: "The whole conception of truth is hard to reconcile with the usual ideals of citizenship [because] . . . it is impossible to instill the scientific spirit into the young so long as any propositions are regarded as sacrosanct and not open to question."[17]

Clearly, then, the relationship between cognitive and affective components of democratic citizenship is not always an easy one. But strain also exists *within* the affective realm itself. First of all, affective ties which predate the polity, both literally and theoretically, may be at variance with the demands of political allegiance. The relationship between the family and the political community (which writers going all the way back to Sophocles in *Antigone* have explored) is only one example of conflicting affective ties and loyalties. In addition, affective ties to those immediately around us, and to local communities, may clash with the building of national and international loyalty. The interdependence of peoples in the world requires the development of attachments to them and to our mutual national and international concerns; but the nature of our affections revolts against a "universal brotherhood" in which we treat all with equal "love." Contemporary proponents of global education (which is gaining greater attention) and the "global community" fail to understand the tensions involved in such a teaching of universal citizenship. They end up promoting a cognitive orientation of (abstract) "love of humanity" or "world responsibility," completely at variance with our affections, memories, and direct experiences, which teach us to prefer those more involved with our immediate political lives. Ultimately the lessons of global citizenship must give way. Benjamin Rush captured the natural friction between local and more universal affection:

> [The student] must be taught to love his fellow creatures in every part of the world, but he must cherish with a more intense and peculiar affection the citizens of Pennsylvania and the United States. I do not wish to see our youth educated with a single prejudice against any nation or country, but we impose a task upon human nature repugnant alike to reason, revelation, and *the ordinary dimensions of the human heart* when we require him to embrace with equal affection the whole family of mankind.[18]

What makes matters even more complicated is that the small scale appropriate to participatory-republican politics contributes to creating the very kinds of local or parochial loyalties which will come into conflict with national or international bonds. The more successful we are at approaching the ideal of participatory-republican citizenship, the more the problem of parochialism will come into play.

To recognize all of the tensions within and between the cognitive and affective spheres of citizenship education is not to propose abandoning one in favor of the other. In fact, these tensions can be treated in themselves as part of the overall education of the citizen, and thereby can be better understood and coped with. If the participatory-republican conception captures our attention as a model for American citizenship, then educators must commit themselves to building both strong cognitive and affective traits in their students, despite the innate problems involved in such a dialectical education.

NOTES

1. See Silberman's discussion in *Crisis in the Classroom,* 7–8.

2. See Henry Giroux, "Critical Theory and Rationality in Citizenship Education," *Curriculum Inquiry* 10, no. 4 (1980): 329–60; Cleo Cherryholmes, "Social Knowledge and Citizenship Education: Two Views of Truth and Criticism," *Curriculum Inquiry* 10, no. 2 (1980): 115–39.

3. Michael Katz, *Class, Bureaucracy, and Schools* (New York: Holt, Rinehart, and Winston, 1975), 31–33. Katz argues that the education of immigrants beginning in the late nineteenth century was aimed at "regulating the feelings and dispositions" of students in order to develop docility, proper deportment, and compliance with the rules of the dominant forces in society.

4. Loyalty, or "the willing and practical and thoroughgoing devotion of a person to a cause," is what Royce feels gives meaning to an individual's life: "If you wholly decline to devote yourself to any cause whatever, your assertion of moral independence will remain but an empty proclaiming of a moral sovereignty over your life, without any definite life over which to be sovereign." Royce sees a definite connection between personal and political meaning, since "to be an object of loyalty, there is then a union of various selves into one life." See Royce, *The Philosophy of Loyalty,* 855–1014—quotations taken from 861, 891, 897, 877, and 874, respectively. This is also Erikson's claim about *fidelity,* in "Youth: Fidelity and Diversity."

5. Paul Goodman, *Growing Up Absurd* (New York: Random House, 1960), 97.

6. Ibid., 231.

7. Samuel Doggett, "A Discourse on Education," in Rudolph, *Essays in Early Republic,* 150–51. For Doggett, the way to get away from this was to fashion an education which would both "inform and direct the understanding" and "meliorate the heart [and] conform the affections."

8. Andrew Oldenquist, "Nature of Citizenship," 30.

9. Roussea, *Emile,* 220–21.

10. Ibid., 220–21, 236, 245. Rousseau's project was to direct the volatile but natural passions to good ends rather than the destructive directions of *amour-propre.*

11. Rousseau, *Emile,* 245.

12. Rousseau argues that "it is less the strength of arms than the moderation of hearts which makes men independent and free." *Emile,* 236.

13. See Wilson Carey McWilliams, *The Idea of Fraternity in America* (Berkeley: University of California Press, 1973), especially 52–53.

14. de Tocqueville, *Democracy in America,* 329–30. Noah Webster felt that affective lessons were *more important* than cognitive ones: "The *virtues* of men are of more consequence to society than their *abilities,* and for this reason the *heart* should be cultivated with more assiduity than the head," in "On the Education of Youth in America," in Rudolph, *Essays in Early Republic,* 67.

15. Royce, *Philosophy of Loyalty,* 884.

16. Mansbridge found this to be the case in close-knit face-to-face associations. See her *Beyond Adversary Democracy,* 34, and also chaps. 6 and 13 for discussion of the dynamics of fear of political conflict in her two case studies of "unitary democracy."

17. Quoted in Fitzgerald, *America Revised,* 209.

18. Rush, "Thoughts Upon the Mode of Education," 14, emphasis added. See also McWilliams, *Idea of Fraternity,* 48–49.

CHAPTER 8

The Role of the Teacher
in Citizenship Education

T HE PRECEDING CHAPTERS have examined the effects of curricula and methods of instruction on citizenship education. The intent has been to identify current curricular practices in the secondary schools and gauge their impact upon the learning of democratic skills and ideals. With the two conceptual models as guides, we have tried to suggest school structures and practices appropriate to a theoretical understanding of what it means to be a democratic citizen.

Integrally related to the curriculum and methods of instruction for democratic citizenship education is the question of the role of the teacher. The teacher, being the dispenser of information, the mediator between child and curriculum, and the practitioner of classroom methods, is pivotal to *any* discussion of educational policy reform. But insofar as the teacher exists in addition as one of the first nonfamilial models of authority and of the "leader-follower" relationship, the role of the teacher seems especially crucial to citizenship education. As mentioned in Part I, the teacher-student relationship has often been seen as the analogue or prototype to that of leaders and citizens in a democracy. Both relationships are ideally characterized by mutual respect, a continuing dialogue over matters of common concern, and development of higher levels of mutual understanding and growth. At the very least, the teacher is the person who can provide the adolescent with many of the intellectual and personal prerequisites necessary for his or her journey from childhood to adulthood, from subject to citizen. This chapter will focus on the role of the teacher in educating democratic citizens. We will initially consider observations about the current dilemmas and problems of high school teachers as a springboard for further examination of competing pictures which exist in educational writing of what teachers and teaching ought to be. Ideas about the proper role of the teacher in democratic political education will be informed by discussions about "teaching" in the tradition of political theory and by the implicit assumptions about the teacher's role in citizenship education contained in the two conceptions of democratic politics and citizenship.

Teachers have increasingly come under fire in contemporary American society. In the past few years the popular press has made the state of teaching in public schools a major source of concern.[1] Parents across the country have come to wonder whether teachers aren't to blame for many of the current problems in public education. They see a decline in student achievement test scores, increasing school violence, and students' failure to learn proper moral and behavioral lessons; many blame these things on teachers' complacency, incompetence, lack of control, and uncaring attitudes. In addition, the alienation of teachers from the community has become stronger over the past twenty years as a result of teacher militancy, unionization, and collective bargaining: many parents are outraged at what they perceive to be the matter-of-factness with which teachers approach their jobs, uninterested and unwilling to put in any extra time to teach their children basic skills and knowledge. One observer argues that the public has come to view teachers solely as "people who work to rule on the basis of agreements embedded in written contracts, and as workers who regularly exercise their right to strike to obtain concessions that more clearly benefit themselves than the students."[2] Furthermore, critics on the left of the educational spectrum like George Leonard also condemn teachers for spending much of their time in "classroom control" and in "damning up the flood of human potentialities," ultimately "preventing the new generation from changing in any deep or significant way."[3]

In earlier times, any community criticism of teachers was muted by the recognition that teachers were better educated than most of the rest of the population. Today much of the general public has become at least as educated as teachers, and sometimes looks upon their profession with contempt; parents often feel that they could and would do a better job of educating their children themselves if they weren't out doing other work that was more important (from society's point of view) and valuable (in financial terms). A 1981 Gallup Poll showed that over two-thirds of American adults felt that teaching was not an attractive career for young people.[4] All of these public attitudes have been shown to have a very strong negative effect on job satisfaction among high school teachers. When teachers are asked about the most crucial problem facing the public schools, they cite most often the lack of parental support, not the lack of student discipline.[5]

The pressure on teachers does not come only from the parents or the community surrounding the school. While teaching is indeed a very public profession constantly open to public scrutiny and criticism, and while parents increasingly are often attempting to exercise their right to influence what goes on in "their schools" (thus threatening teacher autonomy and professionalism), more debilitating to teachers is the pressure which comes from inside the school itself. Within the school, teachers are caught between the needs of students and the demands of school administrators, leading Herbert Kohl to argue that "being a teacher is being smack in the middle of the social system of the school."[6]

Bureaucracy and bureaucratic administration in secondary schools have increased along with their size and problems. The demand for institutional order that has occurred as a result of such burdensome levels of bureaucracy in contemporary schools has reduced the teacher's once highly personalized authority to his or her current role of "mere bureaucratic functionary."[7] Teachers have little input into either the overall curriculum or the school schedule, and are often asked to teach from a preordained set of instructional materials and to administer standardized rules and tests of educational achievement. Most administrators do not reward teachers for curricular innovation or for meeting the learning needs of divergent students, but are interested solely in keeping discipline and order. Where teachers do have some input, in the making up of day-to-day lesson plans, many establish a routine and stick to it as if it were written in stone, thus reinforcing the overall bureaucratization of teaching. Even teachers willing to innovate find that time constraints make impossible the preparation and research necessary for innovation.[8]

Recent educational reforms have further bureaucratized the teacher's place in education. The university-based reforms of the 1960s, most notably the "new social studies," inquiry learning, and some of the proposals for computer- and television-assisted instruction, had as one major intention the bypassing of the classroom teacher, who was felt to be an obstacle to "true learning." These programs all tried to construct "teacher-proof" classroom materials which could "speak directly to the child," thus stimulating individual student interest and exploration. The teacher was to become the mere dispenser of materials or the technician in charge of making things run smoothly, thus moving away from a central role in the educational process.[9]

The new panaceas of "competency-based teacher education" and "teacher-competency testing" also tend to routinize teaching. Here, in response to parents' concerns that teachers are not competently teaching their children basic skills, school boards and colleges of teacher education have begun to prescribe "competencies" to be rigidly fulfilled and implemented by teachers. The resulting emphasis on prescribed outcomes and bureaucratic rules to which teachers must conform tends to destroy the idea that there is any uniqueness to the relationship between teacher and students, or that the process of active dialogue between teacher and students is a worthwhile educational outcome in and of itself.[10]

In addition, government regulation accompanying various educational programs, student-rights litigation in the courts, and teachers' overarching concern with discipline over any other classroom matter all contribute to a school atmosphere in which teachers feel best advised to "stick to the rules" of the institutional order. In summary, one writer contends that "teaching has been pushed in the direction of becoming less an activity in which an informed practitioner exercises professional discretion based on a repertoire of possible actions, and more one that emphasizes routine and direction by rule."[11]

In short, the situation high school teachers find themselves in today is precarious. Held in low esteem by members of the community at large, whom teachers see as holders of an "unlimited warranty" on the "commodity" they sell;[12] treated by administrators as "workers organized for purposes of efficient production," there to enforce rules and administer uniform materials and methods;[13] caught in a conflict in the classroom between the fear of losing control and authority over students and the hope of being their friend and intellectual co-explorer;[14] given poor physical and psychic surroundings and little time for reflection, research, or rest; teachers are increasingly opting out of the public schools.

A National Education Association survey in 1981 showed that over half of the teachers polled said that they would leave teaching before retirement, with 20 percent wanting to leave as soon as possible. More than one-third (36 percent) said that they would not go into teaching if they could start all over again.[15] The number of teachers with twenty years or more experience has dropped by half in the last fifteen years. Furthermore, there has been a decline in intellectual quality among teachers that stay: those with the highest measured academic ability (especially women, who can now command better jobs outside the teaching field than they could before) are leaving teaching more readily than others.[16] Those who do stay suffer from "teacher burnout," stress, fear of student attacks, and the exhaustion caused by being on "the firing line" day in and day out. Rampant absenteeism among teachers is also a growing problem.[17]

None of the current trends in teaching or in the teacher's instructional role bodes well for the education of democratic citizens. The observed decline in active personal relationships between teachers and students not only deadens student interest in learning classroom civics lessons but also fails to generate the kind of interactive spirit necessary to democratic political life. As we saw above, adolescent students need interaction and confrontation with the teacher in order to come to grips meaningfully with their society's knowledge and culture. This kind of relationship cannot occur when teachers are removed from an active role in the learning process. Moreover, the bureaucratization of education created by school administrators "discourages innovative behavior" in teachers and tends to mandate an "absence of intensity" and "promote ineffectiveness and docility" in both teachers and students. The bureaucratized classroom fails to provide the kind of passionate, controversial, and participatory milieu most conducive to the creation of future democrats.[18]

All the factors of the contemporary public high school discussed above lead to a focus on order and management: the "main goal" for the teacher has become "keeping order while conveying a bit of information."[19] One can hardly wonder why there is passivity, alienation, ignorance, and a lack of respect for authority among young citizens when one looks at the current condition of teaching and teachers in the public schools.

The "Traditionalist" Solution

Many educators see the solution to the current crisis in teaching as a return to the hierarchy and discipline of a traditional relationship between student and teacher. Given the unruliness of students and the unmanageability of the classroom which they argue has followed from various child-centered approaches to the teacher's educational role, back-to-basics proponents and others feel that something like a "vertical transmission model" of teaching is the best way of meeting society's educational objectives for its children. Students are more likely, these thinkers say, to learn the basic skills and the values they currently lack, such as respect for authority, when their teachers reassert their positions of mastery in the classroom and go back to "teaching" (rather than coddling) their students.

We have already observed, however, that this traditionalist model of the teacher-student relationship is ultimately detrimental to citizenship education in a democracy. The teacher who feeds already digested and interpreted information and ideas to passively receptive students is not likely to create the kind of active participation and critical awareness essential to democratic citizenship. Critics argue that such a teacher-student relationship will only produce the most shallowly held civic beliefs of patriotism and loyalty, and will not even generate the kind of student interest necessary to the proper learning of school subject matter.

Teachers who assume a hierarchical role of complete control over the progress and evaluation of students, over what happens in the classroom and how it happens, become in effect the student's first "boss," not the paradigm of the "democratic leader." Dewey contended that any educational regimen consisting of "authorities at the upper end handing down to the receivers at the lower end what they must accept" was an education "fit to subvert, pervert, and destroy the foundations of democratic society."[20] Even a conservative like Michael Oakeshott feels that "the activity of the teacher is specified in the first place by the character of his partner," necessitating a view of the teacher's role in civic education which pays serious attention to the child's needs and interests as well as those of the society which wants to bequeath to him or her its "history of human achievements, feelings, emotions, values, and beliefs."[21]

The "Liberationist" Response

But the alternative model which flows from a criticism of the traditional teacher's role in the classroom is also problematic in terms of citizenship education. Current responses to a traditional model of the teacher-student relationship have tended to place the student's individual educational needs and interests at the center of the question of the teacher's proper role in the educational process. Advocates of such alternatives as media-assisted individual instruction, and of open schooling and deschooling (as discussed above), all have sought to bring students into direct contact with educational environments and experiences which would respond to their particular needs. These radical innovators conceive of the teacher's place as being outside the learning process. The teacher is seen as a mere facilitator of the child's own felt educational interests. Roland Barth summarized the role of the teacher in open schools as follows:

> The role of the teacher in an open school is to facilitate learning—to provide conditions which will encourage children to learn for themselves and to fulfill themselves, personally, socially and intellectually. The teacher is not responsible for passing on to children his own knowledge or someone else's knowledge; instead he helps each stu-

dent to find truths inherent in his experiences and to evaluate and revise these tentative truths in the light of subsequent experience.

The open school teacher becomes a "travel agent" in the individual student's educational journey, "available and accessible" but not "interfering" or "dominating."[22] Deschooling advocates like Illich want to stop "funnel[ing] educational programs through the teacher" and instead establish nonauthoritarian "networks of learning." Similarly, followers of Marshall McCluhan propose to make a "casualty" out of "the whole business of teacher-led instruction" through the use of televisions and computers.[23] In the model of the teacher's role (or non-role) based upon these variations of a completely child-centered instructional method, any teacher-initiated activity is justified only if it comes "in response to the native inclination of the student." Teachers are to be teachers "only when and where and insofar as *the student authorizes us to be.*"[24] The vision here is of students learning directly, liberated from the teacher's illegitimate control, with their own perceived educational needs and rights inviolable by the authority of the teacher.

This liberationist model of teacher-student relationships has severe problems as a model for the training of democratic citizens. Of course, by withdrawing from a dominant (and domineering) role in the learning process, the liberationist teacher allows students the freedom to pursue knowledge in their own style and at their own pace. This is a great advance on the traditionalist model, which denies children any authority in their own education. But while open schools and nontraditional learning environments do relieve the teacher of the burden of being omniscient and all-powerful, thus opening up the possibility for him or her to be a partner or co-learner in the classroom (which may be more psychologically conducive to democratic education), these alternatives do not fulfill the promise of liberation for teachers. In attempting to avoid some of the pitfalls of a traditional teacher's role in the classroom, many liberationist educators avoid proposing any authoritative (as opposed to authoritarian) role for the teacher, and some go so far as to bypass the teacher altogether. By declaring that the direct consent of the student is the basis for interaction with teachers as authorities, liberationist educators have failed to formulate a model of the teacher's role which can cultivate students' capacities for equal and cooperative relationships as citizens, or instill respect for necessary authority.

In an educational setting paralleling democratic authority structures, mediation and interaction would take place between students and teachers in a collective classroom setting, not in a setting where individuals decide upon and execute their own learning program isolated from teachers and other students alike. The teacher's role under the liberationist model becomes one of abdication rather than of democratically granted authority. Even Jonathan Kozol, an advocate of "liberation" in education and teaching, is critical of this vision of the teacher as "accidental resource person":

> It has become a commonplace, among too many idealistic converts to the cause of school reform, to speak of themselves as if they were not teachers any longer, but some sort of "incidental person" who just happens to be present among children in the school. Apart from the fact that sensible parents will react with great uneasiness in the face of meandering resource persons with this aimless point of view, there is also the fact that educational abdication of this kind rapidly drives a class into exhaustion—and the nation as a whole into a state of mind which now begins to rally under the banner: back to basics.[25]

These two visions of the teacher's role in education arising from most of the contemporary educational literature, in many ways reflect the two poles of the liberal conception of political education. Both the traditionalist and liberationist models of teacher-student relations in the classroom find support among liberal thinkers. As we have seen in Part I, the teacher as traditional authority figure, who vertically transmits knowledge and values to the impressionable student, is a model which Locke presents in his educational writings. Locke felt that society could best inculcate its norms and customs in future generations through a hierarchical structure in which fathers and teachers unilaterally handed down knowledge and habits of behavior and enforced their acceptance in students through a system which doled out "esteem and disgrace." Locke saw students as passive receptacles of social opinions and habits, as inert elements which the teacher would bring to "a state of knowledge." Under a Lockean conception, the teacher was to be in complete control over the educational process, and discussion or conflict between teachers and students over social and political lessons was to be held to an absolute minimum.

But the liberationist model of the teacher's role in education also lies at the heart of much of liberal political theory. The liberal conception of politics holds individuals to be free and independent, entering into authority relationships only when and where it is in their interest to do so. This view befits an educational vision in which students are seen as autonomous learners, pursuing their own felt instructional needs however they see fit. The stance of the teacher in an open school setting is like that taken by the liberal political order—existing as a facilitator of interaction or experience necessary to enhance the further happiness or success of the individuals who comprise it. The teacher's activities on the behalf of students (as is the case of the liberal polity toward its citizens) is based upon consent, which can be withdrawn when submission to authority's direction no longer meets the individual's needs and interests.

The dichotomy in the liberal conception of psychology, politics, and education which we discussed in detail in Part I is embodied in today's teachers and educational thinkers, who have come to feel that no viable role for teachers remains, between the "old-time tyranny" of the traditional classroom and the "innovative abdication" of the free school.[26] As Dewey argued of many educational reformers at the beginning of this century, today's school practitioners can "conceive of no alternative to adult dictation save child dictation."[27] The result for democratic citizenship of this duality in conceptions of teacher-student relations is frightening: we have the vision of the student-citizen either as a passive, obedient subject or as an uncompromising, uncooperative, tyrannical little child.

An Alternative Model?

Another tradition in the history of political thought suggests an alternative vision of the teacher's role in the education of citizens, somewhere between the extremes of the traditionalist and liberationist models. This tradition goes all the way back to Socrates, who, in *The Republic,* is highly critical of the Thrasymachean method of teaching. Thrasymachus wants to present truths to his students in a speech, and then leave without teaching his lesson in any depth or exploring its ramifications through listeners' questions.

Not unlike the modern practitioners of a "vertical transmission model" of teaching, Thrasymachus ultimately plans to give the student's "soul a forced feeding."[28] Thrasymachus is interested only in speaking to students and ruling them; he does not want to listen to their concerns, obey their instructional needs, or pay attention to the give-and-take of the educational process.

In opposing this method, Socrates contends that what is taught must not only be true and valuable, "but must employ terms with which the questioner admits he is familiar."[29] This means that the teacher must not impose knowledge upon students but must start with their own knowledge and opinions of the subject at hand. But the Socratic teacher does not end here, passively accepting the student's views as sacred. The teacher proceeds from the students' opinions and needs and through dialogue and opposition moves them to a higher understanding. For Socrates, the good teacher acts like a "flat stingray," "provoking" and "perplexing" students by asking questions and posing problems.[30] The teacher begins a process by which, while dumbfounding students about what they previously *believed* to be true, moves them in a mutual endeavor with the teacher to search for and find higher levels of understanding. Throughout, the teacher's role is not directly to "infuse" knowledge into students, but to engage in a mutual dialogue which will slowly turn the student toward the light of understanding.[31] According to Socrates, the good teacher (like Aristotle's good citizen) must know how to rule students and be ruled by them in turn.

Rousseau's *Emile* also represents a dialectical approach to the teacher-pupil relationship. Some dynamics of the teacher's role in his[32] student's education as presented in *Emile* have already been discussed. We have seen that Rousseau opposed both a hierarchical and a purely laissez-faire approach to teacher-student relations. He was highly critical of those tutors intent on maintaining their dominance and superiority over students, and was contemptuous of those teachers who, "in order to play wise men, run down their pupils, affect always to treat them as children, and always distinguish themselves from their pupils in everything they make them do." In contrast, Rousseau advised teachers to "make [students] your equals in order that they may become your equals."[33]

Rousseau, like Socrates, was also opposed to a teacher's unilateral initiation of all lessons based solely upon his or her own opinion of what constitutes a proper education. He felt that to disregard the student's concerns and interests (on their own terms) is to defeat the entire purpose of education, as the pupil's interest and trust, so essential to any learning, are thus broken down. Rousseau cautioned teachers about this disregard:

> If at the child's question you seek only to get out of it and give him a single reason he is not in a condition to understand, he will see that you reason according to your ideas and not his and will believe that what you tell him is good for your age and not his. He will no longer rely on you, and all is lost.[34]

According to Rousseau, it is important for the teacher willingly to admit his own failings and weaknesses to his students in the course of instructing them. The teacher should defer to the child's own curiosity and desires when trying to stimulate his interest in any given subject. This does not mean that he advocated abdicating responsibilities to the student, however; Rousseau argued that teachers should attempt to *create* interest in students where none was originally present. He felt that teachers should provide information or opposition in order not only to satisfy their students' intellectual desires, but to move them beyond where they began their inquiry. He characterized the teacher's role in this way:

> It is rarely up to you [the teacher] to suggest to him [the student] what he ought to learn. It is up to him to [desire] it, to seek it, to find it. It is up to you to put it within his reach, skillfully to give birth to this desire and to furnish him with the means of satisfying it.[35]

Through his relationship with his pupil, the teacher can teach the importance of humility and an understanding of one's own limitations as well as the necessity for assertiveness and self-respect, of feeling equal and independent as well as dependent upon others for assistance and guidance. In this way, the student learns important lessons in democratic psychology. According to Rousseau, the role of the teacher and the relationship he or she promotes with students are critical to the development of persons who consider themselves neither masters nor slaves, but fellow citizens.[36]

John Dewey was also a proponent of a dialectical approach to the role of the teacher in the education of future citizens. We have already noted Dewey's opposition to the "static, cold-storage ideal of knowledge" and to the hierarchical relationship between teacher and student which followed. He felt that this traditional method of relating to students promoted passivity and apathy rather than the kind of activity and autonomy he believed citizens should have, and that it depressed student interest and the critical thinking faculties necessary to proper learning.

But Dewey also took issue with other progressives of his time, who saw the teacher as no more than a facilitator in the educational process. Their emphasis on direct experience as the major source of a student's learning drove many progressives to exclude the teacher from an active role in the individual student's education. Dewey, however, felt that basing education on experience meant that there was a greater role to be played by the teacher (as a mature partner in the educational process), since experience involves the interaction of the individual with her or his environment, including the human environment. Though he saw the role of the teacher as drastically different from that of the traditional lecturer or supplier of information, he believed that the teacher was still a vital element in the student's educational experience:

> The principle that development of experience comes about through interaction means that education is essentially a social process. This quality is realized in the degree in which individuals form a community group. It is absurd to exclude the teacher from membership in the group. As the most mature member of the group he has a peculiar responsibility for the conduct of the interactions and intercommunications which are the very life of the group as a community. . . . When education is based upon experience and educational experience is seen to be a social process . . . the teacher loses the position of external boss or dictator but takes on that of leader of group activities.[37]

As a "leader of group activities," said Dewey, the teacher is not the supplier of ready-made ideas, "pouring in from without" lessons which the student "absorbs like a sponge."[38] Instead, the teacher should actively challenge the student's own thinking and understanding by posing problems, and should attempt actively to direct student experience in directions he or she deems useful while at the same time paying attention to the "characteristic needs and capacities of the student" based on the student's accumulated prior experiences.[39] A mutualistic relationship between teacher and student such as Dewey outlines actually blurs the rigid distinction between teacher and student, since the teacher becomes a co-participant in the process of solving educational problems: "In such shared activity, the teacher is a learner, and the learner is, without knowing it, a teacher."[40]

This composite model of the teacher's role in education presented by these three political thinkers and educators may offer a viable conceptual alternative to the attitude of abdication or coronation which reflects most contemporary educators' approach to teacher-student relations. Democratic citizenship education, like democratic politics, depends upon teachers who neither invade their students' intellectual world and manipulate it, nor passively adapt to students' desires and aspirations, but instead share in the give-and-take of the educational process: alternatively directing or heeding students as they see fit. James McGregor Burns, in drawing a parallel to democratic leadership, outlines the proper function of teachers:

> Teachers—in whatever guise—treat students neither coercively nor instrumentally but as joint seekers of truth and of mutual actualization. They help students define moral values not by imposing their own moralities on them but by posing situations that pose hard moral choices and then encouraging conflict and debate. They seek to help students rise to higher stages of moral reasoning and hence to higher levels of principled judgment. Throughout, teachers provide a social and intellectual environment in which students can *learn*.[41]

In fact, the role of the teacher in political education as presented under this dialectical model closely resembles that of the leader in democratic politics under a participatory-republican conception. Rousseau saw the role of the legislator (or political leader) as being much like that of an educator, bringing follower-citizens to a position where they can be politically self-directing: because "individuals see the good they reject [and] the public wills the good it does not see [,] all stand equally in need of guidance." By helping to constitute and build the "body politic" to "maturity," Rousseau's leader-legislator provides a "public enlightenment" which leads to "the union of understanding and will in the social body," and makes good democratic government possible. Rather than disenfranchising citizens by substituting his own "more enlightened" activity for theirs, the Rousseauvian leader acts to "transform each individual" into a citizen capable of democratic political interaction.[42]

Like the participatory-republican leader, the teacher is conceived by Burns as being a "taskmaster and goal setter" in an environment where both teacher and students are understood to "share a particular space and time, a particular set of motivations and values." As such, the relationship between teacher and students involves "the reciprocal raising of levels of motivation rather than indoctrination or coercion."[43] The teacher's authority, like that of the participatory-republican leader as conceived by thinkers such as Rousseau, is transient and ultimately is based not on the teacher's substituting his or her own "more enlightened" ideas and activities for students', but on the teacher's ability (as an authority figure) to wither away with the growth of the educational authority of the students. The teacher's authority, like that of the democratic leader, is real, but it is based on a commitment to transform itself into a relationship where students who have become more responsible for and capable of equality and autonomy in the learning process interact with teachers as mutual learners, each side operating on the basis of interdependence and mutually imposed restraints in their common quest for higher understanding. Teachers under this conception are committed to the ultimate freedom and equality of their students, but are not willing to abdicate their active role in assuring student progress toward this goal.

One major problem today is that, like modern political liberals in their approach to leadership, many contemporary educators recognize no distinction between authority and tyranny in the classroom. As a result, they tend to divest the teacher's role in the classroom of all substance, fearing a despotic imposition of control or direction upon free learners. But in thinking this way, contemporary educators forget that *democratic authority* of the kind just articulated is the very mean that undergirds a democratic political community—a mean between the "anarchy with a constable" which typifies educational liberationist thought and the kind of authoritarian power proposed by traditionalists.[44]

What does this dialectical model of the teacher's role in education imply for contemporary practices in citizenship education in the high schools? First of all, it suggests that the teacher should assume a more active role in the classroom as a problem poser and challenger of student's critical thinking capacities. Teachers who behave like Socrates's "flat stingray" to challenge students about what they know and believe will be encouraging intellectual debate and growth as well as an active attitude toward the world around them, all of which are important to good citizenship.[45] Active, challenging teachers will also establish critical attitudes in their students toward texts and other instructional materials (see chapter 4).

Teachers must be willing and permitted to innovate in their classroom methods and materials, moving away from the pedagogical extremes suggested by either a traditionalist or liberationist view of teaching. It also means that the kind of student participation both inside and outside the classroom discussed previously as part of the civics curriculum should also be encouraged as a way of providing students with the responsibility and authority promised by a dialectical model of teacher-student relations.

A more active role for the teacher requires that administrators and curricular planners bring teachers into direct and meaningful participation in the formulation of the secondary school curriculum. A founder of a progressive school in Denver has argued that "no program of studies will operate that has not evolved to some extent out of the thinking of the teachers who are to apply it."[46] A recent study contends that "good high schools" are ones where administrators encourage teacher autonomy and initiative in the everyday running of school programs.[47] It must be realized that the bureaucratized or routinized teacher will not be the agent of an education befitting active democratic citizenship.

Teachers also need to re-establish a more cooperative relationship with the communities they serve, with each side understanding the legitimate role the other plays in assuring that the young get a proper education. For too long both teachers and parents have maintained an adversarial relationship; teachers have attempted to insulate themselves from parental control and parents have attempted to protect their children from what they saw as the harmful or illegitimate influence of teachers. Educational institutions such as community school boards and teacher unions have tended to perpetuate this unhealthy relationship.

Of course, this general discussion is not meant to gloss over the specific problems of contemporary secondary school teaching which were outlined at the outset of this chapter. Teachers' concerns about student discipline, administrative and community support, and a proper professional environment (allowing for reflection and discussion) must be addressed. Furthermore, whether teacher-competency testing becomes accepted or not, a method has to be provided to ensure that those coming out of colleges of teacher education know and can teach the basic skills and methods of their content area, and that those in the profession continue to learn new methods and approaches. As we mentioned earlier, future citizens in a democracy need to possess a knowledge of the basics in all areas as well as the participatory values and attitudes that go along with them in constituting complete citizenship training.

The big problem here is that in enforcing competency standards, communities and the legislators who represent them tend to confuse standards with standarization; they hold teachers accountable only for developing students' skills to certain minimal levels. In addition, the regulation of teacher and student competency may further demean the occupation of teaching, by indicating to the teacher that the public has little confidence in the profession. Any attempt to address this question of competency in civic education, then, must consider these problems as well. Of course, some of these problems can be attributed to teacher education programs, which one observer has characterized as lax, unrigorous, and "mainly dedicated to perpetuating their monopoly" over teacher training.[48] Most teacher education programs overemphasize practical training and apprenticeship in training student-teachers, and neglect important "interactive" and "pre-active" components to teaching—and this reinforces the trend toward routinization and bureaucratization in teaching. Moreover, the fact that many elite liberal arts colleges have dropped or are dropping their teacher education programs may not bode well for the development of teachers who understand the importance of an integrated curriculum for the education of citizens.[49]

These specific problems notwithstanding, the incorporation of a more dialectical model of the teacher's role in citizenship education into a conception of secondary schooling which includes the curricular innovations suggested above should assist in revitalizing the high schools as centers of civic learning. Active, Socratic teachers will increase student interest in school subject matter and bring a more democratic order to the classroom, conducive to instruction in the skills and ideals of citizenship. Without these substantive changes in the role of the teacher, the curricular innovations considered critical to training "complete" citizens could not be fully implemented. The republican tradition in political thought has always held that a renewal of decayed public institutions needs founders and leaders who can arouse the public to their renewal. Similarly, the revitalization of the curricular content and institutional structures of democratic citizen education requires teachers who can carry out the new program successfully and inspire the "student-populace" of the schools to learn the new content of the curriculum.

It is no small coincidence that alternative models for the teacher's role in civic education can be found readily in the writings of political theorists. Of course, I have argued throughout for considering the writings of political theorists in thinking about the practical ways in which we educate citizens in America. But with respect to the proper role of the teacher in civic education, the wise words of political theorists seem especially trenchant. The vision of the political theorist as a transmitter of a continually growing tradition of discourse—dialectically challenging and yet building upon what has been handed down from the past—may in fact be the model for the teacher of democratic civic education. In the republican tradition, the political theorist has always stood at the conjunction between founder-leader and educator. It is the theorist's role to challenge the political norms and practices of present generations in light of ideals and examples from other societies and from the past, as well as from the hopes for a common future. The civics teacher, like the political theorist, is an interlocutor in an ongoing discourse which he or she brings to students and conducts with them, challenging students to examine themselves and the world around them, and participating in a mutual quest for greater understanding. The teacher understood as "political theorist" holds great promise as a model for the education of future citizens in a democratic America.

NOTES

1. Cover stories have appeared in all three of the major national news magazines: "Why Teachers Fail," *Newsweek* (September 24, 1984), 64–70; "Teachers Are in Trouble," *Newsweek* (April 27, 1981), 78–84; "Help! Teacher Can't Teach!" *Time* (June 16, 1980), 54ff.; "What's Wrong With Our Teachers?" *U.S. News and World Report* (March 14, 1983), 37–40.

2. J. Myron Atkin, "Who Will Teach in High School?" *Daedalus* (Summer 1981): 100. See also David Selden, "Teachers and Community: Partners or Enemies," *Journal of Education* (August 1976): 31–47.

3. George Leonard, *Education and Ecstasy*, 1–7.

4. Cited in "Teachers Are in Trouble."

5. The most recent Gallup Poll of teacher attitudes toward the public schools is found in *Phi Delta Kappan* (October 1984): 97–107. See also Boyer, *High School*, 154.

6. Herbert Kohl, *On Teaching* (New York: Schocken Books, 1976), 131.

7. Richard Gross, "The Social Studies Teacher: Agent of Change?" *The Social Studies* (July/August 1976), pp. 147–151.

8. Boyer, *High School*, p. 155.

9. Silberman, *Crisis in the Classroom*, 181–82.

10. See Gary Sykes, "Contradictions, Ironies, and Promises Unfulfilled: A Contemporary Account of the Status of Teaching," *Phi Delta Kappan* (October 1983): 87–93.

11. Atkin, "Who Will Teach," 99–100.

12. Sanford Reichart, *Change and the Teacher* (New York: Thomas Y. Crowell, 1969), 57.

13. Oliver, *Education and Community*, 20.

14. See Herve Varenne and Marjorie Kelly, "Friendship and Fairness: Ideological Tensions in an American High School," *Teachers College Record* 7, no. 4 (May 1976): 601–614.

15. Cited in Boyer, *High School*, 159.

16. Phillip Schlechty and Victor Vance, "Do Academically Able Teachers Love Education?" *Phi Delta Kappan* (October 1981): 106–12.

17. See Beatrice Gross, ed., *Teaching Under Pressure* (Santa Monica: Goodyear Publishing Co., 1979), 2–46. The first national conference on "teacher burnout" was held in 1980.

18. See Jonathan Kozol, *On Being a Teacher* (New York: Continuum Publishing Corporation, 1981), 16–20; Bob L. Taylor, "Is Citizenship Education Obsolete?" *Educational Leadership* (February 1974): 246–49.

19. Atkin, "Who Will Teach," 98.

20. Dewey, *Democracy and Education*, 133.

21. Michael Oakeshott, "Learning and Teaching," in R. S. Peters, ed., *The Concept of Education* (New York: Humanities Press, 1967), 156–176.

22. Barth, *Open Education*, 106.

23. McCluhan and Leonard, "Global Village," 106–15.

24. Theodore Roszak, "Educating Contra Naturam," in Gross and Osterman, eds., *High School* 64–65; Herbert Kohl, *On Teaching*, 29–30.

25. Kozol, *On Being a Teacher*, 112.

26. Ibid., 114.

27. Dewey, *Experience and Education*, 18.

28. Plato, *Republic*, pp. 13–23. Here the "object of instruction" is Socrates himself.

29. Meno, in *Plato: The Collected Dialogues,* Hamilton and Cairns, eds. (Princeton: Princeton University Press, 1961), 358.

30. This metaphor is found in Meno, Ibid., 363.

31. Ibid., 381–382. To use the metaphor of the cave, Socrates wants to turn students gradually toward "the light of the sun" and help lead them toward it. By engaging in dialogue, in a give-and-take with students, and by taking their own opinions seriously as the first step in elevating them to higher levels of knowledge, Socrates acknowledges that the power of knowledge is in each soul (in different degrees, of course), to be drawn out and nurtured. The teacher begins with the understanding that the "power" of understanding "is in the soul of each, and that the instrument with which each learns . . . must be turned around from that which *is coming into being* together with the whole soul until it is able to endure looking at that which *is.*" The art of teaching is "an art of this turning around, concerned with the way in which this power can most easily and efficiently be turned around, *not an art of producing sight in it.* Rather this art takes as given that sight is there, but not rightly turned nor looking at what it ought to look at, and accomplishes this object." Thrasymachus, on the other hand, wants to shine the light of the sun directly on the "sightless souls" in the cave, imposing his knowledge upon students "as though . . . putting sight into blind eyes." See Plato, *Republic,* 197.

32. In talking about Rousseau, it is impossible to maintain a gender-neutral syntax, since Rousseau is talking solely about male teachers and male pupils. Still, there is a more universal ideal of the teacher-student relationship contained in Rousseau's writings that is applicable here, regardless of Rousseau's own sex biases.

33. Rousseau, *Emile,* 246.

34. Ibid., 179.

35. Ibid. There are contradictory elements in the teaching in *Emile,* however. The kind of blatant manipulation of the student and the environment with which he interacts with the teacher suggests here that what Rousseau advocates is merely the *appearance* of freedom and mutuality. In reality, Emile's tutor often exercises dominion over him.

36. The teacher is also important because, though Rousseau prefers impersonal law to personal authority in directing the affairs of communities, he feels that law is ineffective in molding people and transforming their attitudes and behavior. Personal authorities in the form of teachers or legislators are needed to activate and "vitalize" impersonal laws in the hearts and minds of future citizens.

37. Dewey, *Experience and Education,* 58–59.

38. Dewey, *Democracy and Education,* 160.

39. Ibid., 183–84.

40. Ibid., 160.

41. Burns, *Leadership,* 449.

42. Rousseau, *Social Contract,* 37–38.

43. Burns, *Leadership.*

44. According to Hannah Arendt, the crisis in democratic authority in modern society has become so acute that authority has even been challenged in "prepolitical" areas such as education. Authority has always been accepted in education, due to the "helplessness of the child" and the political need to guide the young "through a pre–established world into which they are born as strangers." But in contemporary times, people have come to question even the ideas of "temporary authority" as the appropriate relationship between teachers and students. For Arendt, this stems in large part from a confusion about the nature of authority in modern society. See Arendt, "What Is Authority?" in *Between Past and Future* (New York: Penguin Books, 1968),

91–141 (quotations from 92); also Arendt, "The Crisis in Education," in Ibid., especially 191–95. Sara Lightfoot's recent case studies of six high schools also suggest that clear authority relationships between students and teachers contribute to a good atmosphere for learning in general; see her *The Good High School* (New York: Basic Books, 1983), 342–50.

45. One of the major recommendations of *The Paedeia Proposal* is that civic learning "can be helped only by teachers who conduct seminars in the Socratic fashion" Mortimer J. Adler, *The Paideia Proposal: An Educational Manifesto* (New York: MacMillan, 1982); see also Mortimer Adler, "Understanding the U.S.A.," *Journal of Teacher Education* (November–December 1983): 35–37.

46. Quoted in Cremin, *The Transformation of the School*, 299–300.

47. Lightfoot, *Good High School*, 333–42.

48. Gene Lyons, "Why Teachers Can't Teach," *Phi Delta Kappan* (October 1980): 108–12.

49. See Phillip Jackson, "The Way Teaching Is," in National Education Association, *Report of the Seminar on Teaching: The Way Teaching Is* (Washington: National Education Association, 1966), 7–26. See also Sykes, "Contradictions, Ironies, and Promises Unfulfilled," 87–93.

CONCLUSION

The Future of Civic Education
in America

THE NEED for a restructured program of high school civic education is great. In light of the fact that our political problems have become more rather than less complex, and that our effective participation in resolving them is required now more than ever, it is imperative that the education which equips citizens to exercise their rights and fulfill their public duties be able to perform the tasks we have set for it. But it appears that in almost all areas, from the articulation of citizen education goals to the conception of the teacher's proper role in such education, contemporary American curricular wisdom and practices in the high schools have failed to satisfy the demands of democratic citizenship.

I have attempted to use two conceptions of citizenship and political education arising from the tradition of political theory to inform my examination of current practices in the schools. My concern has been to examine school policies regarding the civics curriculum, textbooks, classroom method, general institutional structure, and the teacher's instructional role, to see if they measure up to implicit standards set by both the liberal and participatory-republican models of political education, and if not, to suggest directions the schools might take to improve.

The most striking general observation that can be made after surveying educational theory and practice is that many aspects of school life fly in the face of both the liberal and the participatory-republican conceptions of politics and citizenship education. School structures and policies with important effects on citizenship education seem to have been implanted and maintained without any reflection as to what it means to be a democratic citizen and what educational system would be most conducive to attaining this ideal. In many areas of high school reform, therefore, what is most needed is clear and sound thinking about the impact of school policies on the character of future citizens, given some theoretical understanding of democratic citizenship in America.

Mere thought about the problem will not be enough, however, because where American educators *have* thought about the ramifications of their practices for citizenship, the liberal understanding tends to be most prominently reflected in those practices and reform proposals. This is a problem because the liberal conception as laid out here does not capture the full picture of the human psyche, politics, or education, nor does it sufficiently represent *American* thinking on the subject of politics and citizenship. The participatory-republican model as laid out here is one that speaks to much in the American political and educational experience, and needs to be revitalized in our educational thinking. In fact, I would contend that merely rethinking our secondary school practices in light of the participatory-republican conception would go a long way toward solving the crisis in American civic education.

But this is only a general impression. It remains our task to render some concrete conclusions about the civics program appropriate to the education of democratic citizens. First, educators need to establish a coherent set of goals for citizenship education in the secondary schools. As we saw in Part II, most contemporary educators have failed to set specific aims for civic education and have tended to circumscribe the citizenship aims of general education, just as liberal-democratic writers have wanted narrowly to delimit the arena of participatory democratic politics. Narrowly utilitarian educational goals have taken precedence over the claims of citizenship in most recent educational manifestos. And though the recently completed reports of the National Commission on Excellence in Education and the Carnegie Foundation go a long way toward pointing out some of the social and political goals of education, they still fall short of providing concrete citizenship goals that can be implemented in the high schools. Moreover, as mentioned above, those who have made public proposals based upon both reports have focused on improving mathematics and science instruction, on establishing minimum standards of literacy, and on developing students' "occupational competence."

The current crisis in citizenship requires that we conceive more broadly of the aims of civic education in schools. Of course, educators must continue to concern themselves with literacy, with the basic skills of computation and objective thinking, and with developing students' occupational competence. These first skills are prerequisites to the kinds of cognitive qualities required of citizens, and occupational competence gives students an "occupational place" from which they can approach the public realm. The individual's stake in the political community, her or his sense of dependence upon others in different occupations, and the particular meaning she or he will attach to political issues all come in part from establishing an occupation.

But beyond basic skills and occupational competence, educators' conceptions of democratic citizenship and what it specifically requires in terms of education must be expanded. Secondary schools need to understand their goals as including not just the development of students who respect law, property, and the opinions of others, but the education of students with a wide range of cognitive and affective skills necessary to participation in democratic life. This might include the goal of developing in students skills and attitudes necessary to direct participation in political affairs, as well as a set of substantive values which underlie our political institutions and procedures (see below).

However important a restatement of the general goals of citizenship education may be, it is the actual civics curriculum which is in most need of rethinking. We have already discovered the extent to which the high school curriculum is in disarray. High schools offer a hodgepodge of unconnected courses, and the lessons of democratic citizenship, when taught at all, are relegated to narrowly defined social studies classes. There has been no attempt to *integrate* the high school curriculum in ways which would meet the needs of future citizens.

If we take the thrust of the liberal and participatory-republican conceptions of civic education seriously, an attempt must be made to bring together the divergent courses and activities of the high school to create a unified "civic experience" for the student. In the social studies curriculum this means that students should be presented with more than simply a parade of institutional and historical facts. As we saw above, a rich integration of history—a thorough history of political ideas and values (as well as actions) and their development in the American context—is imperative to any notion of citizenship education. I also argued for the inclusion of a communications component to the social studies curriculum in the high schools. All the basic knowledge of American political history and institutions will not produce competent citizens unless students are also taught the verbal reasoning skills necessary to present their opinions and engage in a dialogue and verbal compromise over issues of common concern. This means that social studies classes should teach students verbal logic and principles of argumentation as well as encouraging debates and "simulated public discussions" between students in the classroom. A solid training in dialogue skills will build both self-confidence and group cooperation in ways that other training will not.[1]

Furthermore, secondary school educators need to rethink their aversion to teaching explicit political values in the classroom. It is clear that educational theorists and practitioners are unhappy with the current state of affairs, hence the popularity of the values clarification and moral development approaches. But these attempts at teaching values become bogged down in the concern that direct discussion of values may involve indoctrination; at their best these methods fail to move beyond the individual level to a development of collective community values.

There is no reason why the basic values which underlie democratic politics cannot be taught and discussed as part of the high school social studies curriculum. Fundamental to democratic citizenship are principles such as democratic equality and justice; a belief in every person's ability and responsibility to participate in public affairs; a concern for the dignity of each individual and her or his personal choices, combined with a dedication to cooperating and sharing experiences; a commitment to resolve public disputes through a process of reasoned debate and conflict *transformation;*

and an attachment to public affairs and to one's fellow citizens. These values need to be made an explicit part of the civics curriculum.

It is true that any explicit value instruction must be cautious of running roughshod over legitimate minority values, especially in a multiracial and multicultural society such as ours. Moreover, there may be an inherent conflict, as mentioned above, between cognitive skills and affective values, or between commitment to a certain set of values and the general belief in openness and toleration that characterizes a democratic society. However, these conflicts in themselves can and should be made a part of the classroom discussion in high school civics courses. Students can be taught the inherent contradictions in and between certain values, and yet be inspired with the importance of being committed to those values which the polity hands down to them and which make future political action both possible and meaningful.

Proposals about the direct teaching of values should not shock contemporary educators. They are already involved in at least the implicit instilling of values, through both the overt and the hidden curriculum of the high school. As a matter of fact, as we saw above, the kinds of values now being taught implicitly may be more dangerous to democratic citizenship and more susceptible to the charge of indoctrination than any program of explicit value instruction. If we take our two conceptions of democratic politics and citizenship seriously, we must realize the importance of inspiring future citizens with fundamental social and political values. It must be remembered that, for liberals and participatory-republicans alike, the political order is held together in part by a common reverence for the same values and ideals, and as such, the conscious instilling of common values is necessary as a foundation for any kind of collective action, either of a conserving or a reforming or revolutionizing nature. Commonly held values are essential to both the liberal goal of enabling individuals to assert their claims *against* the polity and the participatory-republican concern with the intrinsically important process of direct participation and common bonding in the public realm.

The preceding discussion only covers the social studies curriculum. My analysis also points to the need to integrate other disciplines into the student's unified civic experience. If we want students to be knowledgeable and capable of making decisions about the wide range of issues which constitute contemporary American politics, we should provide them with a broad-based secondary school education which includes the sciences, literature, and the arts as well as history and government. This means that teachers in all high school disciplines must be aware of the connections between their particular lessons and desirable civic skills and attitudes. A conception of the curriculum which tries to integrate learning in preparing responsible citizens may require English teachers (at least in part) to assign literature containing political experiences which can be discussed and related to current social and political dilemmas. Art and literature classes might contain discussions about the parallels between the development and applications of standards of taste and judgment in art and in politics. Science teachers could be more conscious of developing students' general observational, logical, and reasoning abilities in ways which link up to the goals of civic rationality and observation. What seems apparent from the current high school curriculum is that students are asked to specialize in their pursuits and to differentiate between various disciplines and approaches, rather than to integrate their educational experiences into a complete whole where connections can be made between art, science, history, and politics. If we want to create better citizens as well as better men and women, this kind of compartmentalized learning in secondary schools must come to an end.

Furthermore, I have also argued that participation both inside and outside the classroom be added to the more formal academic elements of the civics curriculum. By including a participatory component in the high school curriculum, educators can overcome the pernicious effects of the "hidden curriculum," and can contribute to the proper formation of democratic skills and attitudes as well as to increased political knowledge.

There are a number of ways to bring participation into a student's educational experience. High school teachers can incorporate a participatory element into the classroom itself, by being open to class discussion and conducting simulated debates, town meetings, or political conventions. Social studies teachers can institute internships in local government and community associations as part of students' course assignments; students would be asked to spend one day a week working in some public institution (mayor's office, police department, municipal courts, county health and welfare offices, local party organization) in lieu of a certain amount of coursework. High school administrators can also facilitate more meaningful participation in schoolwide policy, by opening up areas of student interest to direct student input. The trend in recent years has been to close off student participation, in response to the increased violence and disorder in the high schools. Possibly, however, making school curricula and institutions more participatory could help remedy the problems of student disorder and violence. There is evidence to suggest that apathy and alienation are major contributors to school disorder, and to the extent that active participation in the classroom and in school decision-making decreases apathy and alienation, the need for force as a disciplinary instrument may diminish.

Student participation can also be increased in community groups which have a direct relationship with the high schools, such as school boards, juvenile law enforcement agencies, and resident associations in the immediate vicinity of the schools. By involving students in these organizations in a meaningful way, students will not only learn important civic lessons but will be united in activity with people from different ages and walks of life (rather than isolated from the world of the community around them as they now are). In addition, if the recent findings of socialization studies like that of Beck and Jennings are correct,[2] student involvement in *any* extracurricular school activities may contribute to improved adult political participation and participatory attitudes. Just by encouraging increased extracurricular activity in all students, especially those from lower-income backgrounds, high schools can help promote greater civic knowledge and awareness along with a propensity to participate in politics in adult life.

My focus in these conclusions so far has been on integrating various elements of the high school curriculum into a unified civic experience for students. But to provide a more complete civic education for future citizens, we must integrate not only courses and activities but also *students* from different backgrounds and interests.

We found earlier that methods of instruction which isolate students from each other and from active interaction with the teacher are not at all conducive to learning the cognitive and affective lessons of democratic citizenship. Proposals for voucher systems and alternative open schools, or the deschooler's "networks of learning," would all have the effect of segregating students according to cultural and religious background or educational interest. The notion that the political community is the place where people come together out of necessity to pursue common goals and solve public problems would be lost in an educational system which encouraged voluntary specialization and a completely child-centered method of instruction.

Rather than looking to create "flashy" structural alternatives, contemporary educators might do better to examine institutions already in place. As discussed above, the comprehensive public high school ideally provides the conditions for future civic life; this is where students can be exposed to a diversity of disciplines under the same roof, and can be brought together with others as equals into face-to-face classroom association. The idea of providing a universal liberal education for all students through the comprehensive public high school—an institution once thought to be the proper educational companion to democratic politics but now in the process of being abandoned in favor of specialized instruction in specialized schools—may indeed be the best answer to the crisis of modern citizenship in America. Educators interested in reviving democratic civic education may want to heed Rousseau's warning that a narrowly specialized or vocational education which fails to round out the student in both head and heart will yield not democratic citizens but people who "remain in isolation with nothing in common save obedience."[3]

The comprehensive public high school as discussed here is, however, only an *ideal* structure for housing a reformed civics curriculum. Restoring it in practice is problematic. Parents today clamor for choice in educational institutions, wanting to provide the best for their children's future. And the relative conditions of public versus private or vocational schools for the most part support their claims. Private schools have been shown to be safer, more orderly, and on the whole productive of higher cognitive achievement test scores in students than the comprehensive public schools.

Many educators as well as parents are calling for more single-purpose, specialized high schools, feeling that it is in the interests both of the individual students and of society to provide institutions which can give accelerated training in specialized fields to students wishing to become experts in these fields. These educators want to replace the comprehensive public high school with what Harold Howe, the former U.S. Commissioner of Education, calls a "galaxy of new institutions yet to be invented."[4] In addition, the current social climate is one in which the individual academic goals rather than social or political goals of high schools are taking precedence, which also tends to reinforce the current trend toward dismantling comprehensive public high schools for more specialized academic alternatives.

In light of this situation, the revitalization of the comprehensive public high schools may be an impossible task. But there are some basic actions that can be taken which might pave the way for their renaissance. First, public confidence in public high schools must be restored if any institutional renewal is to occur. Parents need to be assured that their children will come out of comprehensive public high schools with the basic knowledge and skills necessary to fulfill personal career goals as well as public responsibilities. The public high schools must show a commitment to providing each student with the basic foundations of a liberal education, and must back that commitment up with competency testing to make sure that students can master basic educational problems.

A commitment to restore public confidence also means that the public high schools must address the question of discipline, which is paramount in many parents' concerns about the schools. As we argued above, involving students in school decision-making and even in the collective enforcement of school rules may go a long way in alleviating the problem of disorder. So can a set of *reasonable* regulations concerning student conduct. But schools must also be willing to strictly enforce basic rules of conduct concerning such matters as physical violence, possession of weapons, and the unnecessary disruption of the classroom. Students unwilling to abide by these basic rules should be permanently expelled from the school community (a step which most public schools have been unwilling to take).[5]

Secondly, federal, state, and local governments need to demonstrate their commitment to revitalizing the comprehensive public high schools. Funding must be restored to those programs which make the public high schools "comprehensive." In this era of fiscal conservatism and budget restrictions, bringing back previously cut and currently underfunded programs in art, music, experimental science, special education, or industrial arts is indeed difficult. But no greater economic and political resource exists than a broadly educated citizenry. Perhaps specific high school programs can look to private foundations or other funding sources in addition to tax-payer dollars to support their goals.

In addition, the government can show its commitment to re-vitalized public high schools by abandoning its support for private institutional alternatives. The goals of democratic citizenship educa-tion are not in keeping with public support for private schooling, and such support is a financial zero-sum game as far as the public schools are concerned. By dropping proposals for tuition tax-credits and educational voucher systems, political leaders will be acting in the long-term public interest (though the politicians' own short-term interests may dictate a demagogic appeal to current public opinion). This governmental action, in conjunction with a restored public confidence in the schools, would make it more financially desirable for parents of all backgrounds to send their children to the public high schools, thus potentially infusing them with new blood and vitality. Though these actions may seem quite minor, together they may stave off the further decline of the comprehensive public high schools and set the framework for the more substantive cur-ricular and structural reforms discussed in Part II.

The formidable problems involved in *practically* reviving the comprehensive public high school bring us once again to the argu-ment about the futility of calling for changes in the schools alone. Many of the factors mitigating against a renewal of the public high schools are part of larger problems in American society as a whole (racial and ethnic conflicts, "white flight" from urban areas, privati-zation of interests, economic instabilities, the decline in local and urban communities), and major changes in society may be necessary before the public schools can respond in the ways suggested here. This does not mean that we must give up trying to work for changes in public schooling. The schools are still somewhat open to change, and may indeed be catalysts in rebuilding an "embryonic community life," as Dewey optimistically contended. This statement by two more recent educational commentators demonstrates the hope that still attaches itself to the public schools as democratic political institutions:

> Public schools are everywhere close at hand and open to all children. They generate valuable debates over matters of immediate concern, and offer a potential for community of purpose that is unparalleled in our society. For all their faults, public schools are probably the most responsive institutions we have.[6]

Hannah Arendt said that "education is the point at which we decide whether we love the world enough to assume responsibility for it and by the same token save it from that ruin which, except for renewal, except for the coming of the new and young, would be inevitable." She saw education as a process of preparing our children "in advance for the task of renewing a common world."[7] We must agree with Arendt that American society is undergoing a crisis in education, especially in the education of its citizens. The challenge to American education is clear. We must rethink the way we go about "the task of renewing a common world" with our young, and change our educational practices accordingly. This is especially true since many areas of American secondary education exhibit so little in the way of reflection on the ultimate goals of learning. Here I have attempted to accomplish just this task, going back to a tradition in political theory of thinking about citizenship and civic education in order to examine what it means to be a democratic citizen, and then pointing out some of the failings of American citizenship education in light of this theoretical examination. If this book has at least shed new light upon age-old questions about democratic political education and assisted in providing some of the answers, then I have succeeded.

NOTES

1. See Newmann, et al., *Skills in Citizen Action*, 33–41.
2. Beck and Jennings, "Pathways to Participation," 94–108.
3. "Letter to Dr. Tronchin, 1758," quoted in William Boyd, *The Educational Theory of Jean-Jacques Rousseau* (New York: Russell and Russell, 1911), 25–26.
4. Quoted in Edward Fiske, "The High Schools: New Shapes for the 80s," *The New York Times* (April 26, 1981), p. 12, col. 28.
5. One school in suburban Detroit has had some success with an experiment along these lines. The administration has threatened students guilty of engaging in violence or possessing dangerous weapons with expulsion from school. Since this policy was instituted, violence and disorder in the school has been drastically reduced.
6. Tyack and Hansot, "Conflict and Consensus," 23.
7. Arendt, "The Crisis in Education," 196.

INDEX

Adams, John, 60
Adler, Mortimer (*The Paedeia Proposal*), 184n
Affective component in civic education: 158–62; defined, 8; under the participatory-republican model, 67–68; related to size of polity, 58–59, 161–62; mentioned, 86
American Historical Association, 89
Amour d'soi and *amour propre*, in Rousseau's writings, 64
Arendt, Hannah, 195, 183n
Aristotle: on leadership, 60; on the importance of dialectic in education, 100; mentioned, 52, 66, 174

Back-to-basics, 136–39
Bailey, Stephen, 100
Barber, Benjamin, 73n
Barth, Roland, 170
Bentham, Jeremy, 21
Berelson, Bernard, 91
Bowles, Samuel, 153n
Boyer, Ernest, 15, 85
Bruner, Jerome, 116n
Bureaucracy: 7; its effect on teachers, 166–67, 168–69
Burns, James MacGregor: on teachers and leadership, 177–78; mentioned, 60
Butts, R. Freeman, 145
Cardinal Principles of Secondary Education, 81–82
Carnegie Foundation Report (*High School*): discussion of goals, 85, 186; broad core curriculum in, 109; required community service discussed, 123
Child-centered approach to teaching, 128–30, 170–71
Citizenship: decline in the cultivation of, 4–5, 15; as defined by liberal theory, 31–32; as defined by the participatory-republican model, 61; and student-teacher relations, 177–78
Cognitive citizen education: 155–57; defined, 8
Coleman, James, 142
Communication skills, learned as part of the social studies curriculum, 100, 188
Comprehensive high school: as a structure conducive to citizen education, 150–52, 192; renewal of, 192–94; mentioned, 82–83
Conant, James: on goals, 80; on the comprehensive high school, 83, 151
Conflict: as the foundation for liberal politics, 23–25; transformation in participatory-republican politics, 53–55; avoidance of in the liberal conception of education, 37–38; absence of in civics textbooks, 102–103; discussion of as part of explicit values instruction, 188–89
Coons, John, 143–44, 153n
Cremin, Lawrence, 87n, 133n
Critical education, 156–57
Curriculum, civics: 8, 11; lack of a history component in, 97; an integrated broader curriculum for citizenship discussed, 108–16, 187–88

Dahl, Robert, 29
Deschooling, its effects on civic education, 147–50
Desires: as the basis for liberal politics, 21–22, 31; as understood by participatory-republicans, 48–50, 72n
Dewey, John: and participatory-republican political education, 62, 66–70; on curricular practices, 96, 115; method of instruction, 128, 130, 132; criticism of "basics" education only, 138; on the role of the teacher, 175–77; mentioned, 13, 173, 195

197